The Front Bench Regulars

Wit and Wisdom from Back Home in the Hills

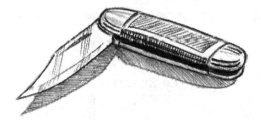

by Larry Dablemont

Illustrations by Tom Goldsmith

The Front Bench Regulars...
Wit & Wisdom from Back Home in the Hills

Copyright 1999 by Larry Dablemont.

Published by
Lightnin' Ridge Books
Illustrations
Tom Goldsmith
Editing and designing
Randy Jones & Lisa Barham
Bolivar Herald-Free Press

ISBN: 0000000000000
LIBRARY OF CONGRESS CATALOG NUMBER:
99-95059

Lightnin' Ridge Books
Box 22, Bolivar, Missouri 65613

TABLE OF CONTENTS

TABLE OF CONTENTS CONT'D

INTRODUCTION

In the 50's and 60's, pool halls had bad reputations. Too often they were places where local ne'er do wells went to gamble, and in some cases there was drinking and bad language. The pool hall you are about to read about had none of that. My dad and grandfather didn't allow that kind of thing. They bought the pool hall in Houston, Missouri when I was about 12 years old. Dad was a factory worker who needed extra income to raise three kids, and there wasn't anything unusual about giving a youngster a job after school to help ends meet. In fact, I always thought dad was giving me a special privilege. He'd sometimes threaten to punish me by making me stay away from the pool hall for a week if I got out of line. Dad didn't have much trouble keeping me in line.

While I was in school, my grandfather opened up and ran the-operation and after school I came in and took over for several hours while dad came home from his factory job, ate supper and rested awhile. Usually, he would let me stay later on certain evenings. When I was there to clean up and close up, there were several old men around to help.

I think I first began to work there when I was 12 years old, and continued until I was about 17. I was obsessed with the outdoors. The nearby Big Piney River and all the fish and wildlife along it fascinated me to no end. And when I found out that most of the old men who came into the pool hall were rivermen and outdoorsmen, that pool hall developed an attraction for me that's hard to explain. Not many 12 and 13 year old boys have friends who are 50 or 60 years older than they, but I did. And there was no gambling and alcohol in our pool hall. Dad didn't allow anything like that, and he made it clear that loud vulgar language would get you an invitation to leave. There was some crusty language at times, but mostly it was toned down when I was around, because those old men didn't want to swear in front of a youngster.

And the front door was always open, sometimes wives and small children came in to watch their husbands and fathers play, or wait patiently while a game was being finished. It was a place where men came to talk about hunting and fishing and old trucks and dogs and guns and farming. It was kind of a home away from home for many of them, and I looked upon them as men of wisdom whom I could learn from. Believe me, I learned a lot.

And I'm sure there are folks back home who will recognize these men I talk about, just by reading about them. They were real people, and a few are still alive today. I changed the names in most cases, because I felt it was better to do that, just in case any surviving relatives might take offense. And I've taken a great deal of journalistic liberty...I can't remember every detail of everything that went on, of course. But by and large, these are true accounts embellished here and polished up there. In some cases, I still remember exact words and phrases, and the expressions on faces as the stories were being told.

I can see them and hear them, and I hope in this book you can also see and hear these old timers my dad affectionately named, "The Front Bench Regulars." This book is a tribute to my old friends who made my boyhood something special. To my way of thinking, they were men of wisdom, every one, and I was one lucky youngster to have been there.

Larry Dahlemont

ii

I OWNED THE PLACE

The Big Piney river flows north through the hills of the southern Missouri Ozarks. When I was a boy, I felt sorry for anyone who lived somewhere else.

The nearby town of Houston was small—a main street with a hotel and restaurant, a pair of drug stores, a hardware, grocery, post office, and courthouse. For folks who didn't like to hunt and fish there was a theatre. And for those who did like to hunt and fish there was a local pool hall where experiences could be relived. Tales of big bucks and bucketmouth bass were told and retold. There were recollections of catfish that couldn't be caught, ridge-running coons that couldn't be treed, and hunting dogs which were legends in bygone days.

The pool hall was situated right at the middle of main street. There were three snooker tables, two pool tables, a soda machine, and a front bench about eighteen feet long, often crowded with old men who became a big part of my world. Old men with overalls and dirty flannel shirts, leathery faces bristling with a three- or four-day growth of whiskers. Old men with tobacco pouches and faded caps to cover bald spots. Old men who were hunters, trappers, fishermen, rivermen and farmers who had the answers to the world's problems if only someone would have listened.

I listened! It became my good fortune to own the place at the age of twelve. My dad and Grandpa McNew were the real owners, but the place was mine.

1

I learned to shoot pool back then, when I was just big enough to lean over the table, and I would have learned to chew tobacco, but dad wouldn't allow it.

It seemed I was the only one among the Front Bench Regulars who didn't. Spittoons sat in a row before the long bench where Ol' Bill, and Herschel Foyt, Virgil Halstead, Charlie Weston, Jess Wolf and Ol' Jim Stallcup told about their adventures on the Big Piney while they watched the main snooker game on the front table.

Winter seemed to wind down slowly in '61. But March tried it's best to come in like a lamb, and Grandpa Dablemont and I were getting our trotlines ready. We'd be going after a big flathead up at the Catfish Rock eddy just as soon as the water warmed a bit. I was pretty excited about that, and it's all I could talk about as the days grew longer, the jonquils bloomed and the tree-frogs began to sing at night

Ol' Bill shook his head as he cut a plug of tobacco one evening and propped one foot on the spittoon. "I seen my last night runnin' trotlines, boy," he said. "If a feller's gonna work that hard, he might as well be married."

"What's the biggest flathead you ever caught?" I asked.

Ol' Bill leaned back and worked on that lump of tobacco, staring at the wall as if trying hard to remember. Then a smile crossed his wrinkled face.

"Don't know if anybody ever tole you this story," he said, "but the night you were born back in....uh...."

"1947," I prompted.

"Yeah, forty-seven it was, I guess," he said rub-

2

bing his gray stubble of whiskers. "Well, that very night me and yore gran'pa was trotlinin' on the Gasconade River, and we caught the biggest flathead I ever seen— 65 pounds I think it was."

"I remember," I said, "anyway I saw the picture of it."

Bill went on, "Well, you don't know the whole story. We brought that big ol' fish up to the feed store to weigh it, and the feller come up from the newspaper to take a pitcher. So me an' yore grandpa ambled right on down to this same pool hall here to do a little braggin'. Course nobody in the pool hall knows a dad-blame thing about the catfish and yore grandpa don't know about his new grandson."

"And didn't care neither," Jess Wolf chipped in from his end of the bench. "Ol' Fred woulda traded two or three grandkids for that big catfish!"

Everybody chuckled at that and Ol' Bill continued. "Well, when we walked into the place that day, right off two or three fellers start slappin' your gran'-pa on the back an' congratulatin' him like he really done somethin'. Natcherly he figgers they heard about the big fish, so he throws out his chest and he says, 'Boys, you can stick both fists down in his mouth side by side'."

Ol' Bill paused a moment to shift his tobacco and wait until the right moment to continue. "Everbody's jaw just drops open a' course," Bill said finally, "cause they don't know a thing about that fish...so yore gran'-pa, he jus' keeps on braggin'. He says, 'took dang near 30 minutes to get that rascal out, cause he was fightin' like the devil hisself'."

" 'Never seed one fight any harder,' he says. Then

3

he says, 'Boys, come next Sunday afternoon, we figger on deep fryin' that big ol' cuss, an' I want you all over to help eat 'im!'"

There was laughter and knee-slapping.....I wasn't sure if there was any truth to the story, but before I could say much more, Jim Stallcup pitched in. "It was a big ol' flathead catfish that cost my cousin his wife and fam'ly," Jim said soberly.

It took awhile, but someone asked how in heck that could be. Jim told about how his cousin loved to noodle catfish, pulling spawning hog flatheads out of hollow logs and such by hand. There was a 55-gallon drum down at the Henry Hayes eddy stuck in four or five feet of water, and Jim's cousin reached in there one evening and grabbed the lower jaw of a flathead the size of a half-grown steer. The fish clamped down on his arm and drug Jim's cousin all around that eddy, with him fighting and kicking the whole time, and the catfish doing the same.

Finally, Jim's cousin wrenched free of the fish and tried to surface, only to find out he had been dragged back beneath the Henry Hayes bluff. Miraculously, he came up in an air pocket, and when he lit his cigarette lighter it was clear that he was in an underwater cave way back under the bluff.

"Well, he climbs up into this cave, gets his feet on solid ground, and starts follerin' this long passageway, just usin' that lighter ever now an' then to see," Jim said, shaking his head in wonder.

"Three days....three days he follers that narrow cave, thinkin' only of that little woman a his, and when he finally staggers out into the light, barely able to go

4

on, he finds out his wife has packed up and went home to her mother."

"Never was able to find that cave again, I don't reckon," Bill interrupted.

"Why no," Jim allowed, "but they ain't no doubt he was tellin' the truth. The boy was still wet, an' his lighter was plumb out of fluid."

"I member somethin' about that," Bill said nodding his head. "Seems like he made the mistake of leavin' his pickup parked over at the Blue Moon Tavern whilst he was down there rasslin' that catfish." When the laughter subsided again, Herschel Foyt said he knew there was a gosh-awful big catfish in that Henry

Hayes eddy, because it had broke his own trotline many times back in the mid-fifties. "Finally, I jus' hung a light nylon rope from a big sycamore limb above the bluff," Herschel said, "and tied me a ice hook right below the water level."

The old farmer had my undivided attention, and everybody waited for him to pull a grape Nehi out of the soda machine and fill it with a penny's worth of peanuts. He took a drink, then leaned against the warm radiator and went on. "I baited that hook right at dark with a banty rooster, just as a big ol' storm moved in. I knew that catfish would prowl that night, an I reckon he did. When that sun peeked over the bluff the next mornin', that sycamore was broke off halfway up, layin' in the river....."

It was quiet, but for the sound of a cue ball ricocheting off the deuce on the front table. Nobody said a word. Finally, I couldn't stand it any longer. "You mean the catfish pulled a tree into the river?" I asked in disbelief.

Herschel took a long swig of soda and looked at me as if I was the dumbest kid in town. "Oh heck no, boy," he said, "Storm blew it down I reckon!"

CHAPTER 2

THE WHUPPED GOBBLER

Ol' Bill didn't seem all that impressed with the return of wild turkeys to the Ozarks. The first season in decades loomed just ahead and he said he didn't know if he'd hunt or not. Ol' Bill had a lot on his mind. The suckers were shoaling pretty good, and smallmouth and rock bass were getting fat in preparation for the spawning season. He said if a feller meant to get serious about spring fishing, it seemed pretty stupid to be hiding in some ridge-top brush pile at daylight, scraping on a box.

For quite some time, grabbing yeller suckers on a Big Piney shoal had been the most popular springtime activity. Now this wild turkey thing could change all that. Ol' Bill didn't cotton much to change of any kind. And he was pretty strong against the idea of paying good money to them conservation people for a turkey tag. Yeller sucker grabbing required no special permits.

Several of the Front Bench Regulars talked it over one evening. Every one of them was old enough to remember when turkeys were plentiful in the Ozarks. Jim Stallcup said the turkeys in the woods nowadays were half-tame, no challenge for a man who remembered the days when they were so wild they didn't even make tracks. He said back then they were too smart to walk on soft ground.

I asked him how many he had called in and killed. "We never did such foolishness back when I was a boy," he snorted. "I'd get 'em off the roost just 'fore daylight, then have the rest of the day to do somethin' else!"

"That's not sportin', Jim," I said. "It's not fair to shoot a turkey on the roost."

Jim looked around him, eyebrows raised in mock disbelief. "I shoot pool for sport boy," he said indignantly. "I shoot turkeys for supper!"

There were a few chuckles, and Ol' Bill put a gnarled hand on my shoulder, shifting his tobacco and pushing his cap back on his head. "What's so sportin' about hidin' in a brush pile an' makin' a noise like a hen turkey that ain't never had a boy friend?" he said. "That kinda thing goes agin' my upbringin'."

"Unfair advantage, I say," Jim was quick to agree. "Imagine me an' Bill here out fishin' an' mindin' our own business, when off down the creek somewhere, we hear some young lady callin' for a good lookin' young feller and allowin' as how desperate she is for courtin'. Why, natcherly we'd amble on down that direction."

"Amble heck," Virgil pitched in, "you'd run like a stripe-tailed jack rabbit."

Before the laughter had died, Jim was pressing home his point—it shouldn't be fair to do such a thing to a poor, dumb gobbler that has spent the last three months sleeping every night on a limb in freezing weather remembering his last good times as a casanova, dang near a year back.

By that time, most everyone on the front bench was sympathetic with the wild turkey gobbler. Most of them could relate to that!

They had me wondering if this turkey hunting was indeed a fair way of doing things. "Still and all," I said, "it doesn't seem right to shoot a turkey while he's asleep in a tree, either."

"Well boy, it's not like it seems," Ol' Bill said. "I ain't roosted a turkey since I was eighteen y'ar old. But they don't just set up there with their heads under one wing waitin' to be shot."

"I tell ya how it use to be," Ol' Jim volunteered. "Turkeys roosted in flocks of 70, 80, maybe more. They was four or five on guard duty all the time. That way most of 'em slept a week 'fore they had to stand watch. When a hunter snuck in tryin' to find a turkey on a limb, he had to be quieter than a bobcat wearin' moccasins. 'Tweren't very often that you could get a shot, an when you did, you couldn't really see where you was aimin'. Most generly, the whole blasted flock would fly off while I was tryin' to figger out where my barrel was. But a turkey hunter knows all ain't lost, ya see, 'cause them turkeys fly ever' direction and light off by themselves, waitin' for daylight. Then they 'member that they talked about what they's gonna do if this ever happened, and sure enough, just after daylight they all come walkin' back to that roost lookin' for ever'body else. And there I sets awaitin'."

"Course that was the way in the fall and winter," Ol' Bill pitched in, "but in the spring, they gets all scattered out. Two or three ol' toms what's been best buddies all winter all of a sudden get madder 'n heck at one another, and they get off roostin' by theirselves, and they is gosh-awful lonely. That's why it ain't real fair to hunt turkeys in the spring."

Verlin Cantwell was shooting snooker on the front table, and he seemed a little amused by all of that talk. "I'm wonderin' if you fellers are just makin' excuses because you can't call up one of those gobblers," he said, pausing to chalk his cue tip and study a difficult shot.

Ol' Jim's eyes narrowed, and I wondered if he wasn't thinking about askin' Verlin to step outside. But Ol' Bill's sense of humor prevailed. "Shucks boy," he said, "back in the spring of '23, I called a gobbler through a forest fire.... scorched off half his feathers and shortened his beard five inches." Verlin didn't hear; he thought everybody was laughing because he scratched on the seven ball.

When I asked Ol' Bill if he'd show me how to use a call, he admitted he was a bit rusty. "In them days, we had an ol' white barnyard gobbler I'd take out and tie up," he said, lifting one foot to rest it on the spittoon. "He'd gobble and gobble, an' pretty soon here'd come a wild gobbler lookin' to whup him. Course it worked good for awhile, but one day a wild gobbler snuck in real quiet from my blind side an' jumped on that ol' white turkey. Course I couldn't shoot without clobberin' 'em both."

"Did he kill the white gobbler?" I asked.

"Naw," Ol' Bill said, shifting his tobacco again, "but by the time I kicked that wild bird off of 'im, he was ruint."

It was quiet again, so I asked impatiently, "Hurt 'im pretty bad?"

"Didn't hurt him a'tall, I don't reckon," Ol' Bill

grinned. "But he was smart enough not to gobble any more when he was tied to a tree. Never was much for huntin' after that."

Ol' Jim allowed as how that old white gobbler would be just the thing for the new turkey season. He said he didn't think a modern-day gobbler could whup a leghorn rooster!

CHAPTER 3

THE MOUSE AND CHIP TRICK

Summer came, and they called a halt to the atrocities comitted in the name of education at the local high school. I was set free and admonished by one teacher to spend as much time at the library as at the pool hall.

I told her I would, but I think we both knew I'd wind up in the library only if my bicycle lost it's brakes on the way to the pool hall and I couldn't make the curve.

It wasn't going to be a summer vacation for me. On weekends, I'd be guiding float fishermen on the river. On weekdays I'd help Grandpa McNew open up the pool hall just after first light and work there much of the time.

Usually I'd work three or four hours in the morning, then take the afternoon off to go fishing down at the Ginseng Eddy, or hunt squirrels in the Tweed bottoms later in the summer. My bicycle had a shotgun or a fishing rod tied across the handlebars most of the time.

Of course, Grandpa Dablemont and I did our share of trotlining, so I didn't work every night. But usually if we weren't fishing, I would run things at the pool hall so dad could be home resting and spending some time with my mom and two sisters. I never could figure why he'd do that. My sisters and I didn't get along at all, and mom made things worse, always wanting me to pull weeds in the garden or help can beans or something.

She was a heartless woman with a mean streak in her that caused me a great deal of difficulty. She expected me to make my bed, bathe regularly, go to church on Sunday, and let my sisters walk all over me.

The pool hall was my refuge. But even more than that, it was a center of learning. Who knew more about fishing and hunting and the river than Ol' Bill and Ol' Jim and Jess Wolf and the rest of the Front Bench Regulars?

One June evening when things were slow, Ol' Bill and I relaxed on the front bench while Jess and Ol' Jim shot snooker on the front table.

"I know what'cha mean boy," Ol' Bill sympathized with me, "seems like a woman ain't happy unless she's miserable."

I looked puzzled by that, so he explained. "You give a woman a chance to go fishin' or squirrel hunting', an' she'll nigh always say she's gotta make some bread or mop the floor or some such nonsense."

"Course, you got to mind your ma boy," Bill said, loosing a stream of tobacco juice at the spittoon. "Onliest fun a mother has is tryin' to keep her youngin' from bein' what he's gonna be anyway. And just as sure as a coon eats crawdaddys, when you get big enough to where your ma can't tell you what to do, you'll marry some young heifer that'll take up where she left off."

I was about to tell Bill that bull frogs would be roostin' in hickory trees before I'd get married, but we were sidetracked when Ev Davis came in totin' an ice

16

chest with a nice smallmouth in it. Ev wasn't much of a fisherman, but he was proud of that brownie; maybe a three-pounder. Said he had caught it on Indian Creek with a minnow just that morning.

Ol' Jim came over and looked at the fish. Leaning on his cue stick, he said he'd caught shade perch dang near that size. Ev resented that and said as much, but he calmed down when Ol' Bill said it might be a record for Indian Creek.

With that, he decided he'd take the fish down to the newspaper office and get his picture made. As the screen door banged shut behind him, I asked Bill if he really thought that might be a record.

"I doubt it boy," Bill said in a low voice as ol' Jim sized up the lay of the table before his next shot, "but I was afraid he'd lop that cue stick over Ol' Jim's head if I didn't say something."

I told Bill about the big smallmouth down at the Ginseng Eddy and allowed as how I didn't think anything could fool that fish. Bill scratched his whiskers and said maybe he'd go after that bass sometime with the old mouse-and-chip trick.

Responding to my bewildered expression, he told me how he had perfected the most deadly fishing technique ever known. He once made a small harness with a treble hook on the back and fitted it to a half-grown house mouse. Then he tied the mouse to his fishing line just like any other lure.

"I took it down to the Catfish Rock hole," Ol' Bill said, "that mouse bitin' an' kickin' an' squirmin' all the way. Just before I chunked him out there I got t' feelin' sorry for the little rascal. So I thought about it awhile, and I figgered I'm faced with turnin' him loose or takin' him home. Either way, he ain't got the chance of a June bug in a chicken house. I figger that this mouse is gonna get it from a cat or an owl or a snake anyway, so why not use his bad luck to catch me a big bass."

I don't think I coulda done that," I said, a little disappointed in my old friend.

"Well, I couldn't either boy," Ol' Bill said, shaking his head. "I throwed that mouse out there and watched him tryin' to swim out. And I knowed he'd drown in just a little while, so I reeled him back in."

"And turned him loose?" I asked hopefully.

"Aw heck no, boy," Ol' Bill answered, somewhat annoyed. "I tied a big chip of wood to the line about eighteen inches above the mouse, and threwed him back out again. Right away, he sees the chip, and he swims over and climbs on it. Then I lets him rest awhile and I jerks the chip out from under him. So he swims for awhile an crawls back on the chip an' I jerks that chip out from under him again. So he swims for awhile an crawls back on the chip an' I jerks that chip out from under that rascal again. I fished for an hour with that mouse an he was swimmin' better an' better. Then it happened."

My heart sank. Somethin' told me that mouse was a gonner. But Bill said no. A big bass made a lightning pass at the swimming mouse and missed, but the six-inch chip lodged crossways in the fish's mouth. After a ten minute fight, the bass was finally landed, and Bill said it was a six or seven-pound largemouth. The chip was lodged inside the jaws so tight he could scarcely get it out, but when he did, there was that mouse, still alive and holding onto the chip with all his might.

I think Bill sensed I was feeling sorry for the mouse. He told me that he took him out of the harness and the little fellow lay there on the gravel bar trying to regain his strength.

"That's when the darndest thing happened," Ol' Bill said shaking his head as he propped one foot on the spittoon. "That mouse kinda pulled hisself together and jumped back in the water. Last I saw of him, just 'fore dark, he was swimmin' aroun' out in the middle, lookin' for that darn chip."

I didn't know how much of that to believe, but I asked if he'd ever tried that again. He said he hadn't. Claimed it was just too much trouble trying to get that harness strapped on a mouse while wearing leather gloves, and Ol' Bill said he wasn't up to doin' it without the gloves....he was just gettin' too old to be mouse-bit for one or two lunker bass.

CHAPTER 4

WORMS

By midsummer it had gotten so hot that we turned on the big fan at the back of the pool hall every morning and left it on all day. But even in the heat, the Front Bench Regulars wandered in every evening to shoot a game of snooker, drink a cold soda or two, and sit around discussing everything from politics and religion to fishing.

Rupert Sims was making good money digging night crawlers down on the Piney and selling them for bait. Rupert was quite a bit younger than most of the Front Bench Regulars, in his mid-twenties maybe. I always thought he was a bit slow, and I had heard Ol' Bill say that Rupert's bait-bucket had a few leaks. But he was doing pretty good that summer digging worms. He claimed he was getting a penny for each adult worm, but the dry weather and heat had driven 'em deep in the ground. He said if we didn't get a good rain in two weeks, he might have to apply for one of those federal disaster loans.

Virgil Halstead pulled a Coca-Cola out of the soda machine and took a long drag on it before offering his opinion. "I had a cousin that used to get all the night crawlers he wanted by drivin' a long steel rod way down in the ground and then beatin' on it with a hammer. Said it just drove them worms crazy, an' they'd come up outa the ground runnin'."

"Holdin' their ears, I bet," Ol' Bill said with a grin.

Virgil thought Ol' Bill was making light of him, so he went on to explain that the same sort of thing had been scientifically documented using an old crank telephone connected to two rods in the ground. He said Bill could poke fun at science all he wanted to, but scientific fact was scientific fact.

"Still and all," Ol' Bill said, "I'd hate to have anyone see me out on the river bank somewhere beatin' on a rod with a hammer, or down on my knees crankin' on an ol' telephone." Rupert didn't see it that way. He said that if it would produce two hunnerd adult worms per hour, he'd pick science over manual labor any day, and danged with what anybody thought.

Jess Wolf had been sittin' on the end of the bench dozing for much of the afternoon. I had already swiped his cap and hidden it behind the soda machine. It was something I did often because Jess was a sound sleeper, and he would sometimes just go on home not realizing he didn't have it. Then the next day he'd come in madder than a riled-up hornet and look for his cap for fifteen minutes. Jess never knew for sure that it was me that took his cap, and I'd try hard to convince him Ol' Jim or somebody else had done it.

Often, after finding his cap, Jess would say that my dad could have done everybody a big favor the night I was born by tying me in a burlap bag with some rocks and dropping me off the Dogs Bluff Bridge.

But Jess was more concerned that night with the science of night crawler diggin', and he asked Rupert how he could tell an adult worm from a juvenile. There were a few chuckles, but Jess was dead serious.

Rupert explained that it was a judgment kind of

thing. He said he just wanted to give young worms a chance at life, knowin' that next year they'd be full grown. "I just sorta calculate by size how old one is," Rupert said, enjoying the fact that his expertise in something was finally being appreciated. "Them big ol' males is the best kind for trotlines," he said, "the females are good for trout and bluegill and the like."

I couldn't believe what I heard. Apparently no one on the front bench knew that worms were different in that matter. Finally, I felt it was my duty to educate everyone. We had studied that sort of thing in science class back in the spring.

"There are no male and female worms," I said. "Last year in school we learned that. They're all the same!" Suddenly I really felt bad...there I was pointing out that none of them was educated.

Then there was a snicker or two, and Virgil Halstead went to shaking his head. "Boy if you was a mite older, I'd have a heck of a lot of questions to ask about that," he said.

The snickers turned to knee-slapping laughter, and my ears got warmer. These guys thought I didn't know what I was talking about. Above the laughter, I tried to straighten it all out. "Earthworms are what they call 'hermaphroditic'. There are no males and no females, each one is both."

It was useless. For ten minutes, everyone made jokes about the situation. I racked the front table and gave Jack Burke change for a dollar as he prepared to play Charlie Weston a game of snooker. I wished I had kept my mouth shut.

Ol' Bill hadn't said much, he just sat there

chewin' an' grinnin'. He winked at me and said, "What's funniest about this is, that boy there has three or four more years of schoolin' than anybody else in here."

"I believe I had an uncle that was a hermaprodil-iac," Herschel Foyt said, "His blood wouldn't clot...they said he'd bleed plum to death if he cut hisself shavin'"

I knew Ol' Bill knew I was right, so I felt some better. But from that point on, I stayed out of the conversation. I racked another table, collected the money, and answered the phone to tell Verlin Cantwell's wife he wasn't there. He was, of course. Seemed like he was always there when she called, but I always had to tell her he wasn't, and she always knew I was lying. It took ten minutes of, "Yes ma'm I will," and, "No ma'm he aint," to get off that phone. I told her finally that Verlin hadn't been in for so long I couldn't hardly remember what he looked like, and just hung up.

Back at the front bench, Rupert Sims was saying that in May he had dug twelve dollars worth of nightcrawlers in four hours. Looking at me, he said with a firm jaw that you didn't dig twelve hunnerd night crawlers in four hours without knowin' the males from the females.

"Personally, I'd pay more for grub worms," Jess Wolf said. "I can't see givin' a penny apiece for somethin' I got under my wood pile!"

"Grub worms are good," Virgil chipped in, "but danged if it don't go agin' my nature to turn over cowpiles all morning just to go fishin' that night."

Ol' Jim Stallcup put in his two cents worth. "Years back," he said, "I guided fer some fly-fisherfeller from St. Louis, an' he had some little ol' hairy bait that

24

was s'pose to imitate a underwater critter he called a hell-ger-mite. Well, he said I could find 'em under rocks an they'd catch fish like nothin' else. But I don't reckon they is any in the Piney. I looked under ever' rock from Sand Shoals to Boilin' Springs an' never found nothin' but bugs."

Finally it was time to cover the tables, turn off the fan, and go home. As the last of the Front Bench Regulars filtered out into the hot July night, I heard Ol' Jim say that catalpa worms were supposed to be good catfish bait.

"I froze some up once in a fruit jar in the ol' lady's freezer, but I never got to use 'em," Virgil said. "They just disappeared."

"Guess your woman throwed 'em out." Ol' Jim said.

"I dunno," Virgil answered as the screen door slammed behind him. "That woman's cookin' all tastes the same...an' I figgered it was best not to ask. I ain't shore they didn't wind up in somethin' I et fer supper.

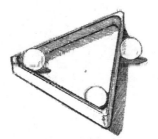

CHAPTER 5

SNOOKER AND MATRIMONY

Old timer Sherman Hawkins had seen much in his lifetime. He fought in World War One overseas, but he didn't talk much about that. He did say he had stood up to the charge of a bear while hunting out west years ago and dropped the bear at fifteen paces. One night in the pool hall, he showed me and Billy Bob Woods the scars on his leg where a wolverine had got ahold of him.

But around the ladies, he was as timid as a mouse. Sherman had never married, and he was getting old enough to wonder if he had made a mistake. Every married man among the Front Bench Regulars assured him he had not, but Sherman had in mind finding out for himself.

He had eyes on the widow Larsen, a sweet little old lady whom he had talked to at church and sat beside once at a revival meeting. He talked big around the pool hall of plans to let the widow know of his intentions. But every time he saw her on the street he holed up in the pool hall and broke out in a sweat. That went on for months, and then they converted an old public building on one end of main street into a senior citizens' center. On Saturday nights, they had a get-together with refreshments and dancing. Dad helped them get an old snooker table brought in from Rolla so they could get more of the old men to come in and feel comfortable.

Well, there wasn't much going on about that

time, with the summer winding down and fall taking its time coming, so several of the old bachelors that hung around the pool hall broke down and went to the senior center one Saturday night. Sherman, feeling a sense of security in a crowd, went along and was standing in a back corner within reach of the punch bowl, making shy-eyes at the widow Larsen. The lady was tired of waiting, I suppose, and she finally decided that if she waited for Sherman to get his nerve up, she'd miss Sunday School the next morning.

So she walked over to him and said, "Why Mr. Hawkins, what a pleasant surprise it is to see you, and isn't it a nice night?" Pawin' around with one foot on the new linoleum, he allowed as how it was a nice night at that, and how he expected the gardens were all gonna burn up if they didn't get some rain. After that he just couldn't think of nothin' else to say. So the widow took the lead again and asked ol' Sherman if he'd like to dance.

Ed Morley was close enough to see it all, and later he gave the details to the Front Bench Regulars. He said that Sherman pawed the floor some more and looked at his feet. His face turned red, and when he looked up, he was grinnin' like a 'possum in a persimmon patch.

"Why shucks Miss Larsen," he said bashfully, "I can't daince a lick." Ed said that at that point, Ol' Sherman's face brightened and his eyes sort of lit up as he spied that empty snooker table in the back.

"But I tell ya what, M'am," he said with a new air of confidence. "Me an' you could go back in the back an' play a little snooker."

Of course the widow had no idea what snooker was. Her eyes got big and her mouth flew open and she turned nearly as red as Sherman's ears. That's when she hit Sherman over the head with her purse. The widow thought she had been insulted!

When Ed Morley first told the story, I believe two or three of the Front Bench Regulars would have rolled on the floor if it had been cleaner. Ol' Bill laughed so hard he started coughing and lost his tobacco. But eventually, when everyone recovered, it got to where there was sympathy for Sherman. The whole week went by and no one saw him. Jess Wolf wondered if maybe he might have gone off down to the Piney and drowned himself.

Preacher Lampkin wondered about that too, and he finally went to have a talk with the widow. He told her what snooker was all about and convinced her that old Sherman Hawkins didn't deserve to be lopped over the head with a handbag for not being a good dancer.

The widow Larsen took it from there. Apparently she went to Sherman with a tearful apology, and the next Saturday night they were at the senior center with the widow learning to play snooker. Sherman took her to church on Sunday and had dinner at her place on Sunday afternoon.

Well, several of the Front Bench Regulars commented in time that you didn't see ol' Sherman at all without the widow anymore. And he didn't have time to come in and shoot pool with his friends, or talk about how bad things were gettin', or speculate about how the quail huntin' would be come fall.

Someone said Sherman had plum quit tobacco,

and Ev Davis said his old pickup had been washed and waxed. Well, it wasn't much of a surprise when word got around that Preacher Lampkin had been asked to unite old Sherman Hawkins and the widow Larsen in holy matrimony.

I recall that evening in September when Ol' Bill and Ol' Jim and Jess Wolf and Virgil Halstead sat around the spittoons with their heads down and their faces somber. They were talking about Sherman as if he were about to be hanged rather than married.

Willie Jenkins was leaning up against the radiator, listening. Poor Willie was about half squirrelly. Everybody knew it and sort of tolerated him. But when he got to asking questions he could drive a person plumb crazy.

"Minds me of a movie I seen once," Ol' Jim said, "Where this ol' sergeant was an Indian fighter for the cavalry all his life. Finally he decides to call it quits after he takes just one more little jaunt with some new feller named Custer."

It was quiet for a minute. Willie was all ears, but finally he couldn't wait any longer. "What happened then?" he asked in his high-ptiched voice. Everybody looked at one another sort of surprised. Ol' Bill grinned and shook his head.

" The same dang thing that's fixin' to happen to Ol' Sherman," he said. Willie had a puzzled look on his face, and I knew he had no idea what the conversation was about.

"I almost got married when I was younger." Jess said, trying to ignore Willie's bewilderment. "But good sense got ahold of me. I started sittin' out two plates ever time I et, an' fillin' both of 'em. Why, it was a sight the passel of good vittles I throwed out in no time at all—enough to feed two or three good bird dogs."

"But Jess," I asked, "you didn't mind feeding your dogs. Why would you worry about how much a wife would eat?" Jess gave me that look they always gave me when they were thinking I was too young to understand, but heck, I was running the place wasn't I?

"Well boy" Jess said, "ever' dog I ever had would retrieve... an' I come to find out that woman wouldn't!" Everybody laughed and slapped their knees and adjusted their caps...everybody that is but Willie Jenkins. He was sort of staring off into space, trying to remember that movie.

Finally it was more than he could bear. "Who did he marry, Jim?" he asked with a sense of urgency. Jim looked at Ol' Bill, and they stopped laughing.

"Who'd he marry?!" Jim restated the question. "You mean Sherman Hawkins?"

"No! no! no!" Willie shook his head in disgust, "that Indian fighter feller......! Who'd he marry?

CHAPTER 6

SQUARL DOG

It was amazing how hot it could get in late September and early October. Just when all the Front Bench Regulars were talking about the upcoming hunting seasons, we'd have that little stretch of 85 or 90 degree weather.

Ol' Bill said it seemed dad-blamed unfair, when a feller had endured the summer and started thinkin' about first frost, and all of a sudden he had to go back to his summer bath schedule...once every four days.

Bill said he measured a summer's severity by the soap he'd used through the end of September, and this year he'd started on a new bar before he spotted his first flight of teal heading south. He said his farm pond had such a soap ring around the bank that the bullfrogs couldn't climb out.

The Big Piney was low, and fishing was sluggish. Jim Stallcup said that in mid-August he had seen a whole flock of turkeys migrating north. Virgil Halstead said it had been so dry that he was findin' seed ticks on the catfish. But the word was that a big cold front would be bringing some rain, so I figured it would be wise to hunt squirrels on Saturday afternoon, despite the heat.

The pool hall wasn't too full that Saturday morning, the front bench almost empty. I heard the screen door slam and turned around in time to see Ol' Joe Throgmorton pulling a little feist behind him on a length of baling twine. The little droopy-eared dog sat

33

there panting profusely, dripping all over the floor.

Ol' Joe didn't give me a chance to ask. "Lookie here boy," he said proudly, "I got me a squarl dog."

As tactfully as I could, I told him I didn't think we allowed dogs in our pool hall. Joe looked awful hurt. He said there wasn't any signs sayin' no dogs, and he had a point. Dad had signs up everywhere: no profanity, no drinkin', no gamblin', no sittin' on the pool tables..but not one sign about dogs.

"Besides that, boy, "Ol' Joe said again, "this here's a squarl dog. Now I know'd you was a squarl hunter, an I thought you'd shore want to hunt squarls with me an' this here squarl dog this e'enin'."

About that time, Ol' Bill walked in. Wiping sweat from his forehead with a red handkerchief, he looked down at the feist and began to shake his head. "What in thunder is that," he growled. It was more of a statement than a question. "Looks like a cross between a house cat and a possum."

Ol' Joe ignored him and with a great deal of enthusiasm he gave me the details of his acquisition. "Got 'im yestiday fer two dollars; might as well a stole 'im. Feller didn't know what he had, I reckon."

"Whoever he was, he came out pretty good," Ol' Bill mumbled as he headed for a cool spot on the front bench, "Made two bucks an' saved hisself a good shotgun shell."

I told Joe I intended to hunt squirrels down at the Tweed bottoms later in the afternoon, but my mom would never let me go with him. Joe wasn't one of the town's top citizens. He hadn't worked since before I was born; he made his spending money by selling pop bottles, and dad said you had to watch him or he'd haul out every empty pop bottle in the place. Ol' Joe wouldn't steal, he figured if the pop bottle was in the empties case behind the front bench it was ours. But out on the floor somewhere, it belonged to anybody.

He wore those old-time black, high-topped tennis shoes, and when he dressed up in his good overalls and clean shirt, he liked to wear an old clip-on tie and a St. Louis Cardinals baseball cap.

Joe rubbed his beard and thought awhile. His eyes lifted as an idea approached him. "I know, boy," he said, "we'll just sorta run inta one 'nother down there at the gate just past the crick. Then you can see how a real genoowine squarl dog works."

That evening, as I coasted down the gravel road on my bike, I could see Ol' Joe's 1939 pickup waiting. The feist was tied to the bumper, scratching at a hard-to-reach flea.

"Had to tie that rascal up." Joe said, "He's jus' too danged anxious. Uh, ain't got a extry shell er two have ya boy? I plum forgot mine."

Suddenly it dawned on me why Joe wanted me along that evening. I had nine shells, and I loaned him three. He promised he'd pay me back come Friday next. "Er, maybe you'd druther wait an' have yoreself the first pup out a this here squarl dog," he said hopefully.

Ol' Joe's gun was in worse shape than his pickup. It was a double- barreled hammer gun with the right hammer broken, so he only had the left barrel to shoot. The winter before he had spied several geese on a neighbor's pond. In his anxiety, he put his shell in the wrong barrel. Figuring the mistake had cost him four

35

or five good meals, he wedged a rock in the chamber of the right barrel. Ol' Joe said by dang he might do something stupid once, but not twice.

Struggling with the twine knot, Joe went on about his new dog. "He's one o' them registrated dogs like they got up north."

Well, the last we saw of him, that's where he was headed...north. We took out behind him, but I didn't count on seeing that dog again. I was surprised when we heard him yapping down the creek. When we got within sight, the squirrel was safely inside a hollow tree, and the dog lit out, scared stiff of Joe's gun, or Joe himself, or both.

"Look at him go, boy, "Joe panted. "He'll have another one dreckly."

He did too, across the river halfway up the hillside. I stripped and took a cool dip in the river. But I told Joe to go on, I'd catch up. I lied about that. Cooled off, I headed back toward my bike. I heard Ol' Joe yelling at his dog once, but I never heard him shoot. Halfway back, I killed a pair of young greys out of one tree, and vowed I'd never hunt with a dog again.

Ol' Joe came by the pool hall that night, long faced and haggard. "Reckon my squarl dog's gone for good boy," he said as he cut off a plug of tobacco and then offered me some to pay me back for the shells. I declined. "Hot dang, he was a goodern too. Couldn't hardly get 'im outa them woods."I figgered I'd best let that ride.

"Reckon a big ol' rattler got 'im, or maybe a wolf. Shoulda had 'im inshored, I spect." A wolf didn't get the feist, nor did a rattler. In church the next day over at

Bucyrus, the McAndrew kids were elated about their new pet, which had almost certainly been Joe's squirrel dog the day before. I knew I should tell Ol' Joe about it, but darn I hated to. I was gonna ask Ol' Bill what he thought I should do, but the problem solved itself.

It cooled off on Monday, and a steady rain started to fall that afternoon. Hot weather was a thing of the past. That evening after school, Ol' Joe rushed in hoppin' with excitement, rain dripping off his cap. "Hot dang, boy, I got us a new squarl dog, an' he's a dandy," he said.

"I don't know Joe," I said, trying to let him down easy. He had three of my shells and he wasn't about to get any more. "I'd just as soon still- hunt for squirrels." A hurt look came across his bearded face as he sank down on the end of the bench.

"It's just hard to keep up with a squirrel dog in that rough country, Joe," I tried to console him. The old man's face lifted and he loosed a stream of tobacco juice toward the spittoon. Wiping a sleeve across his face, he shook his head. "Not this'n boy," he said cheerfully. "He's only got three legs!"

A couple of the Front Bench Regulars ventured out into the rain to take a look at the squirrel dog in the front seat of Joe's pickup, and I heard him tell them as they went out the front door..."might as well a stole 'im, danged feller didn't know what he had!"

CHAPTER 7

THE WHISTLIN' DEER HUNTER

In Big Piney country, the month between Thanksgiving and Christmas was one of my favorite times of the year. By that time all the hunting seasons had opened, and the Front Bench Regulars spent hours telling stories of their experiences. It got dark early, the pool hall was full most of the time, and I always noticed that everyone seemed in a pretty good mood.

Ol' Bill wasn't a bit happy about the passing of deer season, though. He had killed a forkhorn buck—the smallest deer Bill had brought home in fifteen years or so, he said. Just after the season closed, he told the whole story in front of a packed bench.

Bill's deer hunting spot was a carefully guarded secret, but it had been infiltrated. "'Bout a hour after daylight, I'm settin' at this crossin' by an ol' loggin' road," Bill told us, "just scared half to death that I'm gonna kill a big ol' limb-rakin' buck before noon and I'll hafta quit, or scared that I'll pass up a six- or eight-pointer hopin' fer a bigger one an' then not see anothern the whole danged week."

Bill took out his sack of chewing tobacco and, with one foot propped on the bench, started carving as he talked. "It wasn't a hour after daylight that I hear somethin'. At first I thinks to myself it's some kinda bird. Then up this ol' loggin' road comes a city feller totin' a rifle an' whistlin' his fool head off. So I jus' sets there, madder'n heck, an' watch him walk on, whistlin' ever' step, redder'n a dad-blamed fire engine with all those red clothes an' cap an' such."

Bill paused to put up his pocket knife and tobacco and chewed hard on the plug he had just cut. Shifting the tobacco, he continued his story. "So I figger this guy is probably gonna go on off an' shoot somebody's billy goat somewhere, and I settle down ready for a buck. Then this doe comes through the woods, wild-eyed an' high tailed, an' not five minutes after, here comes this city feller back, whistlin' louder an' harder then ever."

There were a few chuckles, but it was plain to see Ol' Bill didn't find much humor in that. "By that time, I was mad," he went on, "so I gets up, an' I step out in the little trail, an' this feller jumps about three feet in the air, still puckered up. I say, 'boy, why the devil are you out here runnin' 'roun', whistlin'! You lost yore dog or somethin'?' Well, he stutters an' stammers a bit, and finally he says he's never hunted deer before, and he figgers if he can scare one up he'll get a shot at it. But finally he confesses that he's kinda worried 'bout some other hunter takin' him for a deer an' shootin' him, so he's been whistlin' his head off fer protection."

"I know'd onc't we started gittin' a deer or two back in this country there'd be them kinda problems,"Ol' Jim said sympathetically. "If I'd a been there, I'd a probly whupped 'im just to set a zample."

A table had to be racked and change given, so I left the front bench for a minute and hurried through the task. On my return, Bill was telling everyone the rest of the story. "...So I say, 'boy I look at it this way. If you come out here an' set down by a stump and wait for a deer, your chances of gettin' shot is one in a million. An' if you come out here an' sneak up an' down some road real quiet, your chances of gettin' shot is one in a thousand. But boy, if you walk up an' down this road anymore, whistlin' like you been a doin', I figger your chances of gettin' shot before dark is darn good.'"

Everybody laughed. But Ol' Bill's problems with the city slicker weren't over. Seems he turned out to be Henrietta Shelton's nephew. Mrs. Shelton lived down the road apiece and was a strong independent woman. Her husband had run out on her years before in search of his own independence. Bill had always fancied himself a good neighbor, so he naturally accepted when the city hunter apologized for being such a greener and asked if Ol' Bill would shoot a deer for him to check.

"I figger it ain't zactly wrong," he said, "specially since the feller has his deer tag and he's sorta scared to go huntin' anyway. An' besides that, he's willin' to pay $25 for the favor."

So two days later, Bill drops this young forkhorn, and he rushes to old lady Shelton's place to find her nephew and tell him he's got himself a deer, gutted and hung up in Bill's smokehouse.

But the neighbor lady says her nephew already has a deer, a nice eight-pointer he shot from a pickup in the field across from Bill's house. "Well they ain't nothin' to do but put my tag on the forkhorn an' take him to the check station," Bill said. "An' that's where I find this kid tellin' ever'body 'round how he set on a deer stand for two days just waitin' fer this ol' hatrack buck, an' how he shot him on a dead run at a hunnerd an' fifty yards."

Bill stopped and sent a spray of tobacco juice toward the spittoon. "Well, he kinda shuts up when I walk up there, an' I told him, 'Young feller, the chances of you gettin' shot by a deer hunter is increasin' by the minute!'"

Again there was knee slapping and laughter, but Ol' Jim never even smiled. From his end of the bench he shook a gnarled finger at Ol' Bill. "Right then is when I'd a whupped him good," Ol' Jim growled. "Jist to make a zample out of 'im."

But the best deer story of the night came later, when most of the snooker players had gone home and only the core of the Front Bench Regulars remained. Pete McGruder, from over around Tyrone, said he was wrestling with a real problem. He had Eugene Pass-

41

more's old single-shot shotgun and didn't know how he could give it back to him without embarrassment.

Finally, he decided to tell it all, hoping Eugene wouldn't get wind of it. Of course, Eugene had never been in the pool hall in his life. He was unmarried, about 30 or so, and still lived with his mother who was one of the richest old ladies in town. Eugene ran his mother's clothing store, and Ol' Bill said he was one of them silk-drawered fellers that went to P.T.A. meetings and played bridge and the like.

Eugene and his mother were big on church going, because Eugene was big in the choir, and it was well known that they were important cogs in one of those "First" churches. 'Course, some of the Front Bench Regulars were church goers too, but most of them went to small country churches that had names like Brown Hill Church or Brushy Creek Church or Ellis Prairie Church.

Ol' Bill said he knew for a fact that there was a First Baptist and a First Methodist Church in every town from Poplar Bluff to St. Joseph, so he knew some of them had to be lying.

Anyway, Eugene was a fixture at the biggest one in the county. He'd walk clean across the street, so's not to walk past the pool hall, and I never saw the man in anything but a white shirt and tie.

Why in the world he decided to go deer hunting, I'll never figure out. Anyway, Pete McGruder said that before daylight on Sunday morning he walked to his deer stand and climbed up into the branches of a big oak that looked out across a small field and pond.

It was about mid-morning when Pete spotted a

hunter clad in bright new hunting clothes walking along the edge of the field. As he grew closer, Pete saw that it was Eugene, carrying that old battered, rusty, single-barrel with the hammer cocked. And as luck would have it, Eugene walked up to Pete's big oak and sat down, leaning the cocked shotgun against the trunk beside him, pointing it up into the branches where Pete sat compeletly undetected.

Pete didn't know what to do. He was kind of worried that Eugene- -a nervous, jumpy kind of fellow anyway—might discharge a round up in the air if he said anything too abruptly. But it became apparent that Eugene had dozed off and was in a deep sleep there, leaning against Pete's tree and ruining the hunting. When Eugene began to snore, Pete could take it no longer. "Eugene..." he said, his deep voice enough to startle the sleeping hunter to full awareness. "Eugene, why ain't you in church!"

Pete said Eugene never looked up and never touched his gun. But he went from sitting still to second gear in one movement and knocked over stumps and uprooted vines as he disappeared into the woods in the general direction of town. I never found out if Eugene made it to church on time that morning, but I'd bet money he was there for part of it.

Pete finally got around to returning the gun by just leaving it in the back seat of Eugene's car. I doubt that Eugene ever used it again, because as far as I know, he never went deer hunting after that. I'm absolutely sure that he never again went on Sunday!

CHAPTER 8

THE ICE GOOSE

Ol' Jim Stallcup shared my love of duck hunting, but he didn't know much more about it than I did. He said sometime he'd like to float down the Big Piney with me and Dad and see if he still had the old touch with a scattergun.

"Did ya ever see a big ol' ice goose, boy?" He asked me one evening in November when I was trying to do my homework. It was early in the evening, and there was just one game of snooker going, so I figured it would be a good time to spread my papers out on the coke machine, pull up a stool, and study hard for ten or fifteen minutes. I hadn't counted on Ol' Jim.

"Kilt the only ice goose I ever seen at Swan Lake fifteen years ago," he went on. "Musta weighed twenty poun's."

"You must mean snow goose, Jim" I said, "I've never heard of an ice goose."

Watching the traffic out on main street, Ol' Jim's eyebrows lifted at that. "Shoot fire boy, I reckon I'd know what I shot. I was there, wasn't I?"

I tried to concentrate on my math but Ol' Jim kept on. "Took that big ol' goose right inta the headquarters there to show 'im off and find out what kind he was, and I'll be hanged if there wasn't a gooseologist there and he..."

"A what?" I interrupted.

"A gooseologist," Ol' Jim said, "a feller that works there studyin' geeses for a livin', finin' anybody that shoots too many an' lookin' over what ever'body shoots to see if they's poor or sickly or how many is he's an' how many is she's."

I put up my books. This was getting a good deal better than the homework. "Why would they care if they were males or females?" I asked.

Ol' Jim reached into his pocket to get some pennies for the peanut machine, giving my question some thought. "Well now, I think that the gooses ain't quite as smart as the ganders," he said, "an' I figger maybe they wanta be sure that the hunters ain't shootin' all of one and leavin' all of t'other."

I didn't say anything, so Jim went on to try to clarify the situation. "Ya see boy, if you got a whole mess of females and not too many males, ever'thing is all right, 'cause the ganders'll take on any extry wives if necessary. Sort of a fatherly instink, I reckon."

As Ol' Jim munched on his peanuts, I tried to visualize the other extreme. "Whad'ya reckon they have when they got only a few females an' a bunch of males," I asked stupidly.

Ol' Jim's face really lit up at that, "Why I don't know boy, but I 'spect the'd have one heckuva good goose fight!" Slapping his leg with his cap, Ol' Jim laughed until I thought he'd choke on his peanuts. Then he leaned back against the radiator and held his sides.

"Maybe that's where they got that sayin', 'Wild goose chase,'." Ol' Jim roared with more laughter. When he finally got a hold of himself, I told him his theory had too many holes. As I understood it from reading all those goose hunting articles in Outdoor Life, geese were thought to be monogamous, mating for life.

"Don't seem fair, does it," Ol' Jim surmised. "The good Lord made ducks and turkeys to chase around from one nest to another somethin' shameful, an' a poor ol' gander gets stuck with one old lady for life."

It was sometime later that I asked Jim once again if he was sure that what he had killed was called an ice goose. "Shore nuff," the old man said. "The feller there at the headquarters weighed 'im and handed 'im back to me, and the last thing he said was, 'Thank you mister, that's an ice goose.'"

By 7 p.m., a half-dozen more of the Front Bench Regulars had ambled in. Ol' Bill was there too, and he was out of sorts, having read about some proposal made for regulating the harvest of ducks by assigning the individual species point values. Everyone knew that would never fly. "Danged point system nonsense," Ol' Bill said, scanning the worn newspaper clipping. "Ah'm agin it."

"Ah'm agin it mahself," Ol' Jim added from the end of the bench. "Jest some more dad-blamed guvamint baloney, that's what it is."

Rubbing his short stubble of whiskers, Bill paid him no mind as he continued to study the piece of paper. "The way I figger it, mallards is gonna be thirty five points, but she mallards is gonna be ninety points, an' wood ducks is gonna be ninety points whether they is a she or a he."

Virgil Halstead and Jess Wolf sidled over to take a glance at the paper clipping, shaking their heads as they found a place on the front bench. "Ain't no ducks anymore," Virgil said. "I 'member when they was all kinds of 'em, gladwells, ballplates, pinwheels..."

47

"How long's it been since I seen black ducks on the Piney?" Ol' Jess pitched in.

"I know where there's some white ducks," Willie Jenkins said in his highpitched voice. "Wonder how many points a white duck has."

Bill just glared at Willie and shook his head. He didn't like to argue with someone who didn't have any powder under his wadding. Willie didn't mind the fact that Bill ignored him. When he was there, he was in every conversation.

"Danged guvamint," Bill said, frowning. "They's only one way to fight 'em, an' that's with money. That's why I'm joinin' this new bunch of fellers tryin' to get the limits off ducks altogether."

"What bunch is it?" Ol' Jim asked eagerly.

"Ducks Unlimited, they calls themselves," Ol' Bill answered. "I'm givin' them a dollar, an' I figger we all oughta give 'em a dollar."

Things got quiet around the front bench. One feller eased out the door, and two others went for the peanut machine. I kind of expected that. They'd join Ducks Unlimited alright, but my dad would be going to P.T.A. meetings before the Front Bench Regulars would fork over any money.

Ol' Jim saw that it was time to get out the billfold or change the subject. "Gettin' colder an' colder," he said as he hauled out his tobacco pouch instead of the money. "Seen a flock of green-wing teal just yesterday." "Well, they ain't worth much," Ol' Bill growled. "The govamint says teal is only gonna be ten p'ints."

"How many of them can you shoot then, Bill?" Ed Morley asked.

"Dadblame it Ed," Bill said, shaking his head as he leaned over the spittoon. "If they's gonna allow a feller a hunnerd points, how many ten point ducks is it gonna take to get your limit?"

Ed rubbed his chin a minute in deep thought and then wandered over to the blackboard to figure. As he was doing that, Virgil came up with an idea. "By golly, Bill, I think I see a bright spot in all this," he said. "That dad-burned game warden prob'ly wouldn't know one duck from t'other."

Bill didn't see any promise in that. "He'll have him a book along, an' even though I 'spect he can't read it too good, he can look at the pitchers an' figger out watcha got."

"Ten of 'em," Ed Morley yelled about that time from the blackboard. "You can shoot ten teals by golly...in fact you can shoot ten of anything that's got ten points."

No one had a chance to respond. Willie Jenkins had been leaning on the radiator trying to roll a ciga-rette. "My sister's husband kilt a ten point deer onc't." he spoke up, intent on his work. "Hit 'im with his truck..."

Ol' Bill leaned forward to stare at the spittoon again, shaking his head slightly. "Danged guvamint," he muttered.

CHAPTER 9

POSSUM IN A BUCKET

Elmar Dinkins told the very first "possum-in-a-bucket" story. It set the stage for more of them, most told in jest really, tall stories that no one expected anyone else to believe. But in February there wasn't much to do but sit around the front bench, shoot snooker on occasion, and tell tall stories.

Elmar didn't mean for anyone to take his story as anything but dead serious fact. He said that he had found a grown possum in one of those empty 55-gallon drums with the lid on tight. The only opening was where there had once been a three- or four-inch cap. Elmar pried off the top of the drum and freed the possum, and he said he had thought about it for years, trying to figure out how that possum could have gotten through that small opening.

Finally it came to him...the possum must have fallen into the barrel when he was very small, and his mama had found him later. Unable to get him out, she had brought him food day after day, and the possum had grown up inside the can.

Of course, since Elmar was a little on the hot-tempered side, nobody came right out and laughed at him. It was plain he believed it all. Later though, everyone had something to say about Elmar's possum story

"I'll bet when he pried that lid off'n that barrel, that possum was about the happiest possum in those parts," Ol' Jim said with a grin.'

"Second happiest," Ol' Bill said. "His mama was happier than he was...bet she was dang near wore out bringin' food to that barrel three or four times a day."

Coach Wilkins may have told the all-time best possum-in-a-bucket story I ever heard. Coach was an intelligent, clean-cut man, and I really looked up to him. He was the only teacher I ever knew that came into the pool hall. Most of the boys my age really idolized Coach, and I never questioned a thing he said. Still, I had second thoughts when he told the Front Bench Regulars how he had floated the upper end of the Big Piney back in the fall and hooked a big smallmouth. Coach waxed eloquent about the fight which ensued, and the huge, black-bodied bass leaving the water in a spray, shaking the lure in a violent attempt to free itself, slinging water every direction in a furious fight for freedom. I felt about half wet just listening to the account.

Later, Ol' Bill commented that listening to Coach Wilkins tell a story made him wish he'd gotten an education. Finally Coach strung the fish on one of those metal stringers, and hung it from a boat seat so it would trail along in the water behind the boat...a heck of a brownie, four or five pounds if it weighed an ounce.

Well, even though he didn't have much more luck, Coach admired that big fish as he floated along, covering mile after mile of river, as the day lengthened. Just a mile or so above the take-out point, they crunched over a rough shoal and the stringer caught on a log. As fate would have it, the big fish broke loose. Coach cussed his luck and moaned all the way to Dog's Bluff, where they were to take out. As they prepared to pull the boat from the water, Coach noticed with amazement that the big bass was right behind it, swimming free. He carefully netted it, and couldn't believe his luck. The broken snap was still embedded in the brownie's lower jaw. Coach said it was the most amazing thing he had ever seen. That fish had just gotten accustomed to following the boat all day, and he couldn't break the habit.

One cold February evening, a handful of the Front Bench Regulars crowded around the old radiator, peering out of the big plate glass window to watch the light snow drifting down past the street lights and they brought up that story in the absence of Coach Wilkens.

"I don't know if I can believe no story 'bout the bass follerin' the boat," Ol' Bill said. "Maybe a twelve-incher would a done that, but a fish don't get to be four or five pounds if he's that dumb."

Of course, I had to defend Coach Wilkins, even though I had some serious doubts about his story myself. "Books I've read say fish don't have a very large brain," I said. "Even a big one wouldn't be real smart."

Doc Dykes, the chiropractor, was shooting snooker on the front table with Satch Himple. Doc also was a well-dressed, clean-shaven, educated man...not really a member of the Front Bench Regulars, but respected and liked by them all.

"You've got a good point there, Larry," he said. "There's irrefutable evidence right here in front of us that getting older and bigger doesn't have a thing to do with getting smarter!"

Ol' Bill glared at Doc Dykes, who had a big grin on his face. I think Bill was wondering if maybe he had-

53

n't been insulted. But Jess Wolf didn't pay any heed. He remembered something he had seen as a youngster.

"One time I was down on the creek when I seen somethin' that showed me right straight how smart a catfish is," Jess said. "They was this little saplin' out in the water three or four feet from the bank, and it was just shakin' like a moonshiner at a tent revival. Well I figger maybe somebody's got a limbline tied on this saplin' an hooked 'em a big ol' catfish, so I sneaks down there to have a look..."

"An steal somebody's fish," Ol' Jim growled from his end of the bench.

Jess took offense, and he stood up to point a crooked finger at Ol' Jim. "That's sorta like a fox accusin' somebody else of watchin' the chicken house." he said.

Doc Dykes was about to sink the five ball in the side pocket, but when he heard that he commenced to laughin' so hard I didn't know if he could finish his game. No one else could figure what Doc thought was so funny. And Ol' Bill, ignoring him, told Jess to go on with his story.

"Well they ain't no limbline on that saplin'," Jess continued. "But there's a big ol' mama catfish, maybe fifteen or twenty pounds, an' she's grabbin' that saplin' an shakin' it jus' like a houn' dog shakin' a snake." Jess really had everyone's attention now...Satch Himple had halted the snooker game to hear the rest of this one.

"Anyway this bush is just plumb full of little ol' bugs an every time she shakes that bush, a mess of 'em falls in the water an' quick as lightnin' fifteen or twen-ty little catfish run in an' eat 'em. Well it really gets

54

to me then, cause it's plain to see that ol' catfish is feed-in' her youngins."

There was a snicker or two on the bench and Satch and Doc were leaning on their cue sticks they were laughing so hard. " That sounds a little bit like Elmar's possum-in-a-bucket story," Ev Davis said shaking his head. Regaining his composure a bit, Doc Dykes said the only thing that could make that story better would be a mama bug diving at that catfish trying to save her own youngins.

Jess scowled, and mumbled somethin' about how a man that couldn't shoot snooker any better than Doc, ought to concentrate on his game. Later that evening, it started snowing a little harder and everyone left but Ol' Bill and Jess and me. I figured dad would be in early to close up .

Ol' Bill said he thought probably Coach Wilkins might have been having some fun with us when he told that story about the freed bass following the boat out of habit.

"You never know," Jess said as he pulled down his ear flaps, "I've heerd it said that sometimes the actual truth is stranger than fact. But I know one thing for shore," Jess was telling him, "A bass just ain't as smart as a catfish!"

CHAPTER 10

THE WAGER

James McNew was one of the Front Bench Regulars, but more of a listener than a tall story teller. He was quite a bit younger than Ol' Bill and Ol' Jim and Jess Wolf and Virgil Halstead. He wasn't a whole lot taller than I was, but as solid as a white oak stump.

Quite often, I'd come into the pool hall feeling my oats and challenge James to an arm-wrestlin' contest. I don't remember how it got started, but we arm-wrestled about once or twice every week with me figuring that eventually I'd get stronger and he'd get older and I'd win. But James probably beat me two hundred times before I went away to college, and then a few times after that when I'd come home on weekends. He didn't seem to get any older!

If I thought I could beat him today, I'd go find James and arm wrestle him again, just so I could say I won once. But I'm not sure I could beat him yet. James was my grandpa McNew's brother's son, which made him a distant relative somehow. You'd think, with me being his third or fourth nephew or something like that, perhaps James would have had some compassion for a thirteen-year-old kid, but he didn't.

One night in front of everyone he said he'd bet me a dollar that he could take me outside and put my thumb in my mouth and I wouldn't be able to come back in without taking it out.

It was the kind of challenge that really gnaws on a person. By refusing to bet, I was making it appear that I wasn't coordinated enought to open a door with one hand. But a dollar was a lot of money at that time, and I hated to risk one when they were so hard to come by.

Ol' Bill recommended that I practice walking in and out with my thumb in my mouth to see if I could do it. And Ev Davis said the whole thing reminded him of the time years ago when Burley Gooch was just a kid, and a travelin' salesman at Venable's store over at Bucyrus bet him a dollar he couldn't eat a whole watermelon all by hisself. Burley was a big ol' strappin' kid, Ev said, but he had apparently been dropped on his head a time or two when he was a baby. Maybe even three times.

"Dropped on his head?" Ol' Bill said with an snort. "Peers to me he was dropped off a high rock into a deep hole!" There were some chuckles about that, as Ev went on to explain that it was plain to see that Burley figured he could win that dollar. He'd walk around in a circle with his hands pushed way down in his overall pockets eyeing that watermelon on Venable's porch, kicking at the gravel with his bare feet.

"Finally he asked if he could run home for a minute," Ev said, "promised he'd be right back. Well the salesman had a good laugh, and he said he figured that big ol' kid woulda tried that melon fer a whole dollar."

"Shoot," Herschel Foyt pitched in, "I allus figgered ol' Burley would eat anything fer a dollar."

"Well he did," Ev said. "He came back and slurped that watermelon down like a hog eatin' grapes. Later after the salesman had left, we was all sittin' aroun' the front porch watchin' Burley flip watermelon

58

seeds off his overalls, when old man Venable says, 'Say boy, where'd you disppear to 'fore you came back and ate that melon.'"

Ev paused a minute to laugh out loud. "Well there he sits with no shirt on, an' watermelon juice all over his face, holdin' that dollar bill like it was the last one he'd ever get. An' he says, 'Wal I went home an' got one a pa's wallermelons an' et it fer practice...wa'nt no doubt if'n I could eat that'n I could eat this'n.'"

The place nearly erupted at that. Several Front Bench Regulars had to get up an' walk around an' hold their sides. But it gave me some courage. After all, ol' Burley had won the dollar.

March dragged on into April and I never stopped thinkin' about that bet James McNew had challenged me to. Ol' Bill and Ol' Jim and Jess Wolf all said it sounded like a safe bet to them; then they allowed as how anybody oughta be able to keep his thumb in his mouth an' get around tolerably well.

But I noticed none of them were jumpin' up to try it. I kept questioning James McNew, but he'd just grin and say if I wanted to find out the particulars, I'd have to put my dollar down. I spent hours in that pool hall trying to figure out what catch there might be and I just couldn't think of any. One thing was sure. If I didn't put up my dollar and call James on it, I'd die an old man wondering what he knew that I didn't.

About mid-April Eugene Passmore, the church choir director, told Hershel Foyt he finally had a shot at a turkey gobbler but he hadn't took it. He said that the ol' tom was sick apparently...it was all huffed up with its head down and wings drooped, feathers ever which away, just barely gettin' along.

Of course every country boy in the Ozarks knew that Eugene's turkey wasn't sick, it was just struttin'. The Front Bench Regulars made sport of 'im for most of the evenin'.

I woulda liked to turkey hunt, but I was busy on weekends paddlin' a johnboat for float fishermen who wanted to catch goggle-eye. I got 50 cents per hour, an' I gave some thought to settin' aside a dollar of it to call James McNew's hand on that bet.

But I usually had more to do with the money I had than I had money to do with. There were three outdoor magazines to buy every month at Herron's drug store, and across the street at the Westside Cafe a piece of pecan pie was 35 cents. I bought one about every two or three days, becoming something of a favored customer at the Westside Cafe.

I could go to the Melba theatre just up the street for a quarter, but I'd wind up spending close to that on popcorn and soda, and I was too busy with my boat paddlin' and workin' at the pool hall to go to movies much anyway. By that time they were runnin' those stupid Elvis Presley movies so much that they hardly ever had time for Randolph Scott.

My extra money went into my savings account in a tobacco can in my drawer...a sort of special occasion fund that ranged from $2 to $3 on occasion.

My big break came when I found a half-dozen good golf balls at the golf course. That was another sideline of mine. There was an old pond past the golf course just off the first tee, surrounded by weeds. I had spent some spare time there, spreading word among the lady golfers that I had seen a snake in that pond that was so long he couldn't straighten out and stay in the water. When they hit a golf ball anywhere close to that pond, it was mine, they'd never look for it!

When no one was playing, I'd go in there and find a half-dozen golf balls in short order. I then sold them for 25 cents apiece to Shorty Evans or Jerald Jeffries, who played snooker and golf both.

So it came about that I had an extra dollar that night in late April when James McNew came in and beat me at arm wrestlin' once again. I could tell by the look on his face that he was surprised when I put my dollar down. I told him that I wasn't the best arm wrestler in the world but I sure as heck could open the door to the pool hall with one hand.

Unfortunately it was still light outside, and a good-sized group of Front Bench Regulars were on hand: Ol' Bill and Ol' Jim of course, Jess Wolf and Jack Burke and Charlie Weston and I can't remember who all.

James didn't fiddle around, he showed me where to stand, right on the curb next to the sign that read "Two Hour Parking." Then he took my arm and put it around the post and told me to open my mouth.

All around, there were old men slapping their knees and roaring with laughter. All pool and snooker games had stopped and from inside I could hear more hoorahin'.

But I was thinkin' of that dollar...I wasn't ready to give up yet. With my thumb in my mouth and my arm around that sign post I stood looking up that pole, wondering if I could climb it one-handed. Gradually,

everyone filed back into the pool hall and I was alone, so intent upon finding a way to get my arm over the top of that sign post, I hadn't noticed anyone else.

Suddenly it dawned on me that folks were stopping and staring. A couple of the waitresses in the Westside Cafe, and Mr. Hayes over at Hayes grocery, were all looking out their windows shaking their heads and pointing. I suddenly realized that my dad could drive up any minute, or one of my teachers could pass by, heaven forbid. The situation had deteriorated. It was time to give up the dollar and try to save some dignity. I took my thumb out of my mouth and leaned up against the post nonchalantly for a moment, arms folded as if there wasn't a thing about it all that was unusual. I could hear more laughter from inside the pool hall.

Eventually I got over being mad at James McNew because he gave me back my dollar. And everybody said I was a good sport about it but I really wasn't. It's just that when you're thirteen you don't have much of an opportunity for revenge.

But I was the kind of kid that learned from his mistakes and I knew I'd do some good with that trick at school. As a result, it seems like I ate more pecan pie for a month or so than I ever had in my life.

LENGTH LIMITS AND CRANES

Normally, there weren't many of the Front Bench Regulars to be found around the pool hall on a Saturday afternoon in May, but one Saturday it was pouring rain and had been for two days. Grandpa and I were going to trotline that weekend up at the mouth of Hog Creek, but the Big Piney was way out of its banks.

64

I reasoned it would be smart to spend the day in the pool hall. Mom had been talking about getting someone to clean out the smokehouse, and I thought maybe she had me in mind for the job.

In some respects, I had a lot in common with those old rivermen when it came to working around the house. So dad gave me the money bag and went home to watch the ballgame, even though I warned him in advance that he'd probably have to clean the smokehouse. He said he'd be the one to decide when that smokehouse got cleaned out and when it didn't!

The rain was still pouring down when dad came back in shortly after he had left. He said the danged Yankees were way out in front and the ballgame wasn't worth watching, so he decided he'd come back and shoot a game or two of snooker.

"Ain't much of an afternoon to clean out the smokehouse," Ol' Bill said with a grin, winking at me.

It made things rough on me when dad was in the pool hall and I was running the place. I had to look like I was really working. There wasn't as much time to sit around and listen and ask questions. And that afternoon they had the big discussion about the proposed length limits on bass in the Big Piney.

Dad and Garnett Sliger, shooting snooker and pitching in every now and then, couldn't figure out why anyone would object to a twelve-inch length limit. Who would want to keep an eleven-inch bass anyway?

Ol' Jim Stallcup pointed out that rivermen like him counted on eating fish out of the river to help out with the grocery bill. "Now you take a four- or five-poun' brown bass," Jim said, "an' he's so dadblamed old he's tougher'n a shake shingle, but if you're wantin' a good mess a fish, them yearlin's jus' melt in a feller's mouth."

"I guess you'd throw back anything over two pounds, Jim?" Ev Davis laughed. "Just too tough to eat."

Ol' Jim detected a general amusement at his position, and you could tell it made him a little hot under the collar. "Heck fire, I ain't sayin' I throw all the big uns back, but my ol' lady gave one to the cat once't an' he couldn't eat it neither." Ev backed off a little, seeing Ol' Jim getting all worked up. After all, the old man didn't have many teeth. Ol' Bill put his two cents worth in at that point. He said by golly he didn't much cotton to them conservation people tellin' him how long his fish had to be.

"Let 'em get this here kinda thing in," he said, "an' by jingo, nex' year they may jus' up an' figger we oughta throw back ever' thing that ain't six inches wide."

"I'm agin' it," Jess Wolf said, "cause ever' now an' then you can catch a big ol' fat bass an' he ain't quite twelve-inches long, an' he's got more meat on 'im than a skinny one that's fifteen inches er so."

Dad paused a minute from his game and tried to point out that if all bass under twelve inches were thrown back, there would be more bass over twelve inches to be caught, and after all, who could argue with that.

Ol' Jim thought a moment, and said that as he saw it, there were better ways to improve the Big Piney. The best thing for fish it seemed clear to him, was to get rid of them dad-gummed cranes. Someday I would learn that the big long-legged "cranes" along the river were also known as great blue herons. Ol' Jim said they were the fish-killin'est creatures on God's green earth.

"One time," he said as everyone listened intently, "I seen one a them cranes standin' in shaller water like he's froze there, jus' lookin' an' waitin'! Pretty soon he stabs that long beak in the water an' comes up with a bass a foot-an-a-half long. Well, I sneaks up close to get a little better look an' I'm hanged if he ain't holdin' down two more with his feet."

Everyone looked at one another, wondering if anyone ought to laugh, but before the snickers got started good, Virgil Halstead pitched in his support for Ol' Jim. "Prob'ly had babies somewhere!" he said. "Bloodthirsty devils!"

"I don't know about cranes," Ol' Bill said, "but if they'd get rid of a bunch of them blasted turtles, they'd save a lot more fish in one year than all of us'll eat in a lifetime."

"Right there's the problem," Jess Wolf said, pointing his finger at no one in particular for emphasis. "Ever'thing eats fish, but nothin' eats turtles or cranes."

Burley Gooch walked in about that time, soaking wet, standing just inside the door like a drowned rat. "I dunno," Ol' Bill said. "Ol' Burley there eats ever' turtle he can ketch."

"I reckon he'd eat a crane too, if'n he could ketch it," Ol' Jim snorted. There was laughter but Burley ignored everyone. He had found a place where it was dry, and he was happy.

I went to rack another table and collect the

money. With the rain, every table was going and the place was really getting packed. Dad finished his game and decided he'd take over for me. I found a spot in the corner next to the Coke box and listened as the debate continued.

Jess Wolf was saying that he thought a big flood like we were having was one of the worst things that could happen to the fish. "I wouldn't doubt one little bit that ever' bass in the river gets washed halfway to the Mississippi by this high water," Jess said.

Bill dug into his pocket for his knife and prepared to cut off a plug of tobacco. "It ain't like that Jess," he said. "Fish sorta grab aholt of limbs an' grass an' hold on 'til the water goes down."

Ol' Jim helped to make the point. "Like chiggers," he said. "Ever notice you can't wash chiggers off with a water hose?"

"Not seed ticks neither," Virgil Halstead chipped in. "Washin' em' off is like tryin' to drown a bullfrog."

Rupert Sims came in out of the rain about that time and was warmly received. He was something of a V.I.P. just about then. The story had gotten around that a few days back, Rupert had been snagging yaller suckers from a leaning sycamore limb ten feet over the Big Piney. The local game warden spied Rupert perched out on that limb, and asked him if he had his license. Rupert said he did, and the warden asked him to climb down and show it. Rupert said he couldn't do that until he caught a few more suckers. The warden figured Rupert was lyin', so he climbed out on that sycamore limb to see the license, and the limb broke with the added weight. Both men went in. They weren't hurt, but Rupert broke the end off his best rod and was contemplating a lawsuit against the game warden.

The game warden, however, had an old fishing rod at home that Rupert took a shine to. And while he was looking at it, the warden gave him some old fishing lures, too. So in short order the two had become friends, somewhat, and Rupert said he'd be willing to teach the warden the fine points of sucker grabbin'."

According to Rupert, the game warden was just as much against that length limit thing as anyone...said it would have him arrestin' every kid and old lady on the river, and he'd probably have to quit goin' to church, lock up his truck at night, and wear a disguise just to go in for groceries.

Ol' Jim, who didn't much trust game wardens, said if the feller cared what folks thought of him, he would have waited until poor old Rupert caught a nice string of suckers and crawled down off that sycamore to check his license. "But no," Jim said, "he had to crawl out there and capsize one of the the best sucker-snaggin' trees on the whole river."

Somebody asked Rupert what he was thinkin' when he heard that limb crack behind him. He scratched his head and thought about it for a moment. "Well," he said, "I 'member thinkin' that this here shore as heck is gonna ruin the sucker grabbin' fer awhile.'"

CHAPTER 12...

PREACHER LAMPKIN &
OLD LADY CANTWELL

There weren't many confrontations in the pool hall, but everyone got a little testy when it got hot and humid in mid-summer. I remember that one time when Ol' Jess said something about one of his cousins having a brother-in-law that could smell quail as good or better than a bird dog.

Ol' Bill was skeptical of that, and he said as much. Jess bristled; after all, it was his relatives Bill was hoorahin'. Usually, Jess and Bill were the best of friends, but when Bill said that anyone who claimed they could smell quail before they cleaned 'em ought to be kept in a kennel and fed dog biscuits, well, Jess took it personal. He jumped up and invited Bill outside, knowing full well that the other Front Bench Regulars wouldn't let 'em go. Somebody said he thought the whole thing was attributable to the recent poor fishing and the fact that the huntin' season was still so far off.

Sitting by the Coke box, I shoved my homework aside and began to read an article in the latest issue of Field and Stream magazine. "With set wings, they fell from the skies as if fleeing the cold north wind," it began, "and the sleet, driven by the norther, stung our faces as we jumped to shoot."

I sighed and dreamed about being an outdoor writer, knowing full well that if I didn't get out of that pool hall someday, I'd never have anything to write about.

About that time the phone rang back toward the rear of the pool hall. It was one of those old time wall phones that you dialed a number on. Up until that time, phones were quite a bit more primitive. You just picked up the receiver and waited for an operator to come on and say, "Number please?" Dad was proud of that dial phone, but most of the Front Bench Regulars were "ag'in it." Ol' Bill had never needed a phone and had lost track of how to use one after they took off the crank and put on a dial. But he wasn't married like some of the younger men who hung around our place to play snooker and they saw the phone as an invasion of privacy. It put them within earshot of their wives, so to speak, during their leisure time.

Verlin Cantwell had the answer to the problem. When the phone rang, he just told me to say he wasn't there if it was his wife calling. Verlin's wife could have climbed on a broom and rode the thing to town, if you get my drift. That woman made life miserable for me because she knew full well I was lying for Verlin. And, of course, I had to listen to her cater-wauling while Verlin nonchalantly worried about whether or not he could bank the five ball in the side pocket.

He would never, ever, take a call from his wife, so I'd finally just have to leave the thing dangling and walk off. You could tell when she finally hung up, because the cord and receiver would just sort of relax. We always thought Verlin's wife would kill him someday when he got home after refusing one of her calls, but he never seemed to look any worse for wear the next day. Verlin Cantwell had to have nerves of steel.

Preacher Lampkin had a piano for sale back in the winter of 1960, and Verlin's wife had wanted one for some time. So Verlin decided to buy the preacher's piano for her, hoping it would shut her up — for a while anyway. Preacher Lampkin was a real preacher, but he didn't have a regular church, so he stopped in at the pool hall on occasion, just to be sociable, against the day he got one. And that's how Verlin heard about the piano.

The preacher was a gentle sort — no match for Verlin's wife. I was busy brushing off snooker tables the afternoon when she called....the same day Verlin

72

was over at the preacher's, closing the deal. Since I was busy, Ol' Bill answered the phone. He listened for a minute and then I heard him say, "Verlin ain't here." Then he stood there and listened for awhile, gettin' red-faced and shiftin' his tobacco. Finally, Bill had heard enough.

"Look, you goosed-eyed ol' battle-ax," he hollered, "I said he ain't here an' he ain't here. He's over to Preacher Lampkins buyin' a..a...uh... uh.... buyin' hisself a bird- dog!"

With that Bill slammed the phone down and sidled back toward the front bench with a grin on his face. Verlin Cantwell had two or three of the most worthless bird dogs in the county, and his wife hated those dogs worse than she hated snooker.

I heard the next day that she had hung up the phone in a rage and driven over to Preacher Lampkin's place bent on keeping Verlin from getting that bird dog. She hit that driveway a little too fast and didn't get stopped in time to keep from planting her De Soto in the flower bed, knocking over a picket fence and a lamp post. I guess it was some sight. I don't know the particulars of what was said or done, but folks said that while Preacher Lampkin didn't actually lose his religion, he strained it a mite. Old Lady Cantwell never did get the piano, and I don't guess Preacher Lampkin ever did get a church. It didn't matter...he had a pretty good congregation there in the pool hall, and not one woman in the bunch.

CHAPTER 13

LIGHTNIN' & BANANAS

The Old Settlers' Reunion and Fair was an extension of the Fourth of July Picnic, an event that was as ancient as some of the Front Bench Regulars themselves. The old-timers talked of the days when folks came in horse-drawn wagons and lived in tents for up to a week at a time. They came from all reaches of the Big Piney watershed—Plato, Roby, Bucyrus, Success, Licking, Tyrone, Solo, and Cabool.

The Front Bench Regulars were old settlers themselves...they settled in the pool hall each evening and talked about reunions and picnics of years gone by.

Ol' Bill recalled that when he was just a youngin' a midsummer storm hit during the reunion and flooded all the creeks. Some folks were unable to get home for several days.

I mentioned that there probably weren't any weathermen back in those days. Before Ol' Bill could respond, Jack Burke put in his two cents worth.

"Heck, when Bill was young, there warn't even any weather!" Jack could get away with that kind of talk. He was one of a handful of people that Ol' Bill liked. Ol' Bill could be awfully gruff with some of the others.

But he could always count on Ol' Jim and Jess Wolf to back him up. If Bill said he "seen it," Ol' Jim could be counted on to say he "seen it too," and Jess would be quick to add that he "seen one just like it."

"I got no use for weathermen," Jess said. "Never noticed it being too hot er too cold, never called off a fishin' trip fer nothin', til them fellers come along."

"Once was a time the only thing a feller had to worry about ruinin' his future was his wife," Ol" Jim said in agreement. "Now you got game wardens an' weathermen."

Preacher Lampkin played the devil's advocate. He pointed out that weathermen were capable of warning people about violent storms that bring tornadoes.

"I aint' much afeerd of cyclones," said Virgil Halstead, "but lightnin' worries me a mite."

Herschel Foyt said he knew a man who had been hit by lightnin' once fishin' for brownies down on Roubidoux Creek. He said the feller had on rubber hip boots and a stringer of fish trailin' behind him. "He seen a big bolt a lightnin' hit the end of his fishin' rod an' he woke up some time after that, layin' flat on his back on a gravel-bar," Herschel said.

"You mean to tell me he got hit by lightnin' an' lived through it?" Ol' Bill asked with skepticism.

"Well, he warn't never the same after that," Herschel said. "Lost all his hair fer one thing, but that ain't the strangest part. Ever' fish on his stringer was fried, and his boots didn't leak no more. Still and all, he never would go wadin' agin. Always fished from a boat after that!"

Ol' Bill wasn't buying any of that. "What difference is they in wadin' an' fishin' out'n a boat in a lightnin' storm?" he asked.

"I dunno," Herschel said, "but they musta been somethin' to it. He never got hit by lightnin' agin!"

Ol' Jim picked up where Herschel had left off and said that he knew for a fact that lightnin' had done some strange things in the past. He gave the details of an old uncle who had been sorely afflicted by rheumatism. He was heading for his cabin to get out of a storm and was astraddle a barbed wire fence when lightnin' hit the fence about a half-mile away. "Course it knocked him fer a loop, but his roomatiz never bothered him agin."

"I believe I knew him," Ev Davis said with a grin.

"Spryest ol' man I ever seen...talked with a real high voice though." Everyone laughed hard except Jim and me. I figured we must've missed something.

Ol' Bill popped another fly with a rolled up newspaper. One thing about the pool hall—there weren't many flies. And with that big old fan on high speed in the back, it wasn't all that hot either.

"I 'member how folks uster could tell what the weather was gonna be by watchin' things," Ol' Bill said. "When flies was bitin', you could always figger on a storm comin'." I asked why that was.

Ol' Bill acted a little aggravated at that. "Nobody knows that. It's some a that science stuff you're always a studyin'. Flies bite afore a storm, fish bite after...rain before seven, sunshine before eleven, that sorta thing."

Ol' Jim took it from there. "When the skies are blue er grey, go fishin' all day; when the skies are green er yeller, head fer the cellar.

"I heard somethin' like that onc't," Jess said. "It went somethin' like, 'Red sky in the mornin' better take warnin', an' red sky at night...'uh..." Jess took off his cap and scratched his head trying to remember.

Ol' Jim tried to help him. "Red sky at night means there's a forest fire somewheres," he said.

"That don't rhyme at all," Bill said disgustedly.

"Makes sense though," Ol' Jim answered.

I went to rack a back table and collect the money. It took awhile. Blackie Sherrill and Verlin Cantwell had played a close game of eight ball, and Blackie said Verlin hadn't called his last shot. I tried to be a peacemaker, but it didn't do much good. Neither wanted to pay the dime. Finally they decided they'd play one more

77

game and the loser would pay for both games. I went along with it, knowing that when the game was over, there'd be another big argument.

Around the front bench, talk had shifted to the Old Settlers Reunion and Fair. Everyone was finding one reason or another why they wouldn't go. Ol' Bill said he thought it was stupid to give a quarter to sit in a box and go around in a circle for two or three minutes and get sick as a mule. Doc Dykes had come in, and he pointed out that it was fun to ride those contraptions if you had a young lady to ride with.

"All I can say is, women must be a whole lot harder to keep happy nowadays," Bill said. "The ones I ran aroun' with back years ago would a druther had the quarter than to get slung all aroun' in a box."

"This here dollar to get in is what I objeck to," Ol' Jim said. "Why, I could shoot snooker all night fer that!" It was customary for the loser to pay for the games, so an eyebrow or two was raised at that. Ol' Jim wasn't that good.

I pointed out that my cousins and I never paid that dollar to get into the carnival. We always snuck through the fence in the back corner. But I couldn't deny that we all paid a quarter to get on the fastest, scariest ride out there. And get sick, just like Ol' Bill said.

It was sort of a test of manhood. My cousins, the McNew brothers, were a tough bunch. They already looked down on me for not smoking cigars or chewing tobacco with them, so if I had to get the living devil scared out of me for a quarter, I'd do it.

The part I was ashamed to own up to was that

Butch McNew and I spent a dollar or better throwing softballs at Coke bottles once, trying to win a dad-blamed teddy bear that neither one of us would have been seen with.

Jess Wolf said he could understand. Carnivals did things to a feller. He told the story about how he had once spent a nickel his dad had give him on bananas at a picnic when he was about fourteen or fifteen years old.

Jess said he didn't realize how many bananas you could buy for a nickel back then, but it was a whole sackful. He had only eaten two or three bananas in his whole life. He guarded that sack as if it were gold, because he had never eaten anything better than a banana, and the last thing he wanted to do was share even one with some undeserving friend.

"I ate most of 'em," he said with a sour look on his face, "but not all. I guess I was sick fer two weeks. But it never had came to me that you could have too many bananas, until that night."

"Now you can't buy more'n a couple fer a nickel," Ol' Bill said shaking his head. "An' I've noticed they ain't near as good as they was back then. It's a dern disgrace the way things is goin'."

I sat there and took it all in, and it would be years before I ate a banana without wondering what it might have tasted like back in the good old days when Bill and Jess and Jim were boys like me.

CHAPTER 14...

SLIM YARDELLE & THE STALLMAN BROTHERS

Slim Yardelle was one of the town sons who had made good in life. He was foreman at the local garment factory, and only a year or so before he had married a lady from a neighboring town that all the Front Bench Regulars agreed was one fine looker.

But it takes more than looks to make a good wife, and in the sweltering heat of August, word was out that Slim and his wife were having trouble, stemming from an unfortunate incident on the Big Piney near the mouth of Brushy Creek.

80

Slim and his young spouse often spent their leisure time fishing for smallmouth on the river, and he had boasted on her progress as a fisherwoman, though as I understand it she had been getting nowhere as a boat paddler. A patient sort, that didn't bother Slim, he could take care of the paddling. About all his wife would have to do is net his fish for him, and that's where the problem developed.

Slim had never caught a really big smallmouth, until that late summer evening on the Big Piney. When that big bass hit, Slim knew he had a prize. There wasn't any doubt that it would go four and a half, maybe five pounds.

With the fight almost over, Slim's wife leaned over to net the fish, unprepared for the last-gasp surge the big brownie would make. When it did, she made a swipe at it, and the rim of the net became entangled with the hooks. A moment or so later, Slim had nothing but an empty net to reel in.

It's hot in August, and it's frustrating to lose a fish. And Ol' Bill said Slim had been under lots of pressure at work. At any rate, poor Slim couldn't take it. There was his wife leaning over the side of the boat, on her knees, peering into the water as if trying to see where the fish had gone. And there was Slim with a boat paddle right in front of him. So he went off the deep end...or rather his wife did, after Slim smacked her with the paddle.

Now Slim was living in a rented house trailer, paying for that one moment of poor judgement. All the Front Bench Regulars were sympathetic, though most agreed he'd be better off single. But the latest word indicated he and his wife weren't any closer to getting back together, and Slim was broke up over it.

"Doggone shame somethin' like that hadda happen to a good ol' boy like Slim," Ol' Bill said as darkness finally settled that August evening.

"Can't help but feel sorry for him," Jess Wolf said.

"Rotten luck all right," Ol' Jim reflected after a long pause. "I reckon that fish was a yard long."

After a certain amount of sympathy had been expressed, the Front Bench Regulars got on to other things. Someone recalled how years ago the Stallman brothers, Lon and Jon, who lived over on the other side of Ellis Prairie, had made a boat out of two old car hoods. That was when a car hood was deep and pointed, and two of 'em welded together made something like a twelve-foot-long, six-foot-wide canoe. The Stallman brothers weren't real good fishermen. They tried to set a trotline once and before it was over, Jon had to have a number six Mustad hook forcibly removed from an area he couldn't reach very easily on his own, and his brother wasn't inclined to help him with. And then Lon had lost some of his thumb once trying to set a bear trap to catch one of the neighbors' free-ranging hogs that had been ranging in his garden.

Hershel Foyt was trying to tell the story about the Stallman brothers and the welded car-hood boat, but on occasion he had to sit down and wipe his face off with a handkerchief and try to stop laughing.

They had put the upside-down welded car-hood boat in the water down at the Plankyard hole just above the mouth of Arthur's Creek and paddled it around awhile with no difficulty, complimenting each other on the boat's river-worthiness.

When Hershel broke down from time to time, Virgil Halstead would pitch in an' help him. Virgil said they had two or three old lard cans inside the "boat" for seats.

Well, one Sunday afternoon, Ol' Jon Stallman decided he'd take his new-found lady friend on a fishin' trip at the Plankyard eddy. She allowed as how it wasn't proper for a lady to go out in pursuit of recreation with a gentleman unless someone else, like his brother for instance, went along. I guess Jon just didn't see that the lady had her hat set for his older brother, so he agreed to take Lon along.

So the three of 'em were there in that old car-hood boat, tied to a half-submerged root wad, sitting on their lard buckets, clutching cane poles, when the lady hooked her very first goggle-eye. The natural reaction, of course, was for all three of the boat's occupants to arise from their lard cans to look over the side of the boat to get a glimpse of the fish. In a split second, the sudden increase in weight to the starboard side flipped the car hoods into their original upright positions, with the three former occupants beneath them.

Fortunately, the water was only shoulder deep, but it was dark there under the homemade boat, and in the process of both brothers trying to rescue the lady in different directions she was personally offended. For quite some time the Stallman brothers wouldn't speak to one another over that.

Jon said that it was his place to rescue his lady friend, and Lon had taken improper liberties. Lon denied it. He said it was dark under there, and he was just trying to gather in those lard cans before they sank.

It was a good 20 minutes before all the laughing subsided. Then Ol' Jim got it going again by telling about how scared the Stallman brothers were of storms. He said that years back, an old farmer down at Strawberry Holler, just east of the Big Piney, had built himself a nice cellar. Down the stairs and through the door, it was hard to see, dark, damp and cool in there, as all cellars are. But from the inside, there were two doors side by side, one leading out and up the stairs, and one opening into a small cubby hole where Old Farmer Welch stored his turnips.

One Saturday afternoon the Stallmans were headed home from town, down past Strawberry Holler to the Sand Shoals bridge which they had to cross to get home. A storm blew up fast, dark and noisy, and Jon Stallman sensed he'd never get much past the Sand Shoals crossing before a cyclone would descend upon them. So he had Lon ask the Welch family if they could hole up in their cellar for a spell to escape impending doom.

Farmer Welch had some neighbors visiting, and he allowed as how it would be best if they all took shelter in the cellar until the storm blew over. So there they were in that little cellar with one old kerosene lantern, the Welches and their youngin's, the neighbors and theirs, and Ol' Jon and Lon Stallman.

I guess it got to blowin' pretty good outside, and Jon got curious to see just how bad it was. So he elbowed his way toward the door, through the ladies and youngins and past one yard dog.

But in the dim light of the lantern, Joe got ahold

of the wrong door handle. Unaware of his mistake, he opened the cubby hole door where the turnips were stored, and peered inside for a moment. With his head still inside, the Welches and their neighbors heard him say, "Hot dang Lon, it's lucky fer us we stopped...it's pitch black out cheer an' smells just like turnips."

CHAPTER 15

BURLEY THE WATER-WHOMPER

Satch Himple and Burley Gooch found some teal on Virgil Halstead's farm pond in the fall of '61. It was a perfect situation, but Ol' Burley cheated a little and crawled up over the pond bank and killed all three before they could get off the water and before Satch could get off his hands and knees.

Satch really got mad about that and spread word among the Front Bench Regulars that Burley was a no-good water-whomper and didn't know the meaning of the word "sportin'."

Burley was a big, rotund fellow that you kind of felt sorry for. He lived with his old parents on a broken down farm over by Eunice, and a good meal was about all he had to look forward to. Somebody said he didn't get fed regular as a youngin because he was so hefty. One time his pa gave him a nickel to go without supper and then took it out of his overalls pocket during the night and wouldn't let him have any breakfast for losing it. Seemed awful cruel to me, but you couldn't tell by looking that he'd ever missed a meal. He didn't work; folks said he was hurt in the army, and a little slow. The only energy Burley expended was in rounding up something to eat."

Satch was sort of sore about not getting a shot at those teal, so he asked Burley how he'd like to come over to his place and have a roast duck dinner. Burley handed over the teal and allowed as how he'd be free that very night.

Satch told everyone he cooked Burley's ducks without removing the entrails. But ol' Burley ruined the joke when he ate everything but bones and entrails, threw the rest on the floor for Satch's dog, and didn't leave until every biscuit and pickle was gone.

Burley didn't seem to mind being scorned as unsportsmanlike for shooting those three teal on the water. He had three ducks, and that was three more than Satch had.

I asked him one evening when things were slow why he shot those ducks sittin'. "Oh, they warn't sittin'," he said, shaking his head vigorously. "They was swimmin' to th' other side o' th' pond. 'Nother five minutes, they'd a been plumb out a range."

"But Burley," I said, "you are supposed to let 'em fly."

"Don't see why," he said. "I intended to shoot 'em...they didn't have no better chance flyin' than they did swimmin'.

I asked him if he was trying to say that ducks on the water had as good a chance as ducks in the air? "Better!" Burley nodded the affirmative. "Lots better chance."

"That's ridiculous, Burley," I said. "How could a duck on the water have any chance at all?"

"They coulda dived," Burley said, with his lower jaw jutting out stubbornly. "That's the only chance they had." Later I told Ol' Bill about what Burley had said, and he laughed so hard he nearly lost his tobacco.

Then he told me about the time Burley had

crossed the river down at Dog's Bluff Bridge and saw a pie-billed grebe out in the river. The "mudhen" looked like a good meal, so Burley took his shotgun and three shells and snuck down as close as he could get. The mudhen dived, of course, and came up about 45 yards away. Burley wasted three rounds of number four shot on that wisp of a mudhen, which slipped beneath the surface at each report and then popped up again, seemingly invincible. Burley didn't tell a soul, but Amil Campbell had seen it all from the bridge, and he said it reminded him of the coyote in that road-runner cartoon at the motion picture theatre.

Bill reckoned that it was the only time Burley Gooch had fired his shotgun three times with nothing to show for it, and every duck from then on would pay for it...unless they dived!

CHAPTER 16

OF TEACHERS AND TRUFFLES

Not many of the things I was exposed to in high school stuck with me, and certainly not much of what I learned would have made much difference to the Front Bench Regulars. They weren't the best educated men in the world, but that's not to say they weren't intelligent. School teachers and rivermen lived in two different worlds....and there I was, a thirteen-year-old kid spending half of a day in one and half of a day in the other.

My teachers never knew how much I learned in that poolroom. Some of them thought it was disgraceful for a boy my age to be in a pool hall, let alone run the place. Mrs. Cranford, for instance. At the time I thought that that old, hawk-faced lady hated me. Looking back, I realize that I was right...she did! She smiled at me only once—while returning a test on which I had completely gone down the tubes. "You might do better young man," she said, "if you spent less time in that pool hall with those ignorant old men!" Of course, we both knew it would have killed her if I had made a good grade. The high point of her career was giving me a "C" each semester. Ol' lady Cranford couldn't paddle a boat, and she wouldn't have known the difference between a goggle-eye and a shade perch. Ol' Bill could have shown her how to set a trotline and she still wouldn't have been able to do it. And she called him ignorant!

Bill sympathized with me, but he told me that it was best that I kept right on pluggin' away and finish school in spite of the teachers. He said he even went to school some hisself. "It's kinda like walkin' barefoot through the chicken house," he said, "You ain't gonna enjoy it, but you can do it if you'll keep your mind on somethin' else."

Doc Dykes was listening as I told Ol' Bill how Mrs. Cranford was continually making life hard on me in school. "I've seen that ol' lady," he said with an understanding nod. "She looks like she could chew a hole in a hog-wire fence."

"Well you ain't heard the half of it," Bill said. "That ol' lady had told the boy here he ought not to be in here 'cause we're all a bunch of igner'nt ol' men. Now how you reckon she come up with that, since she ain't never been in here?"

"I don't know that she would have to come in here to figure that out," Doc said with a smile. "She could have just asked someone!"

"There you go agin, callin' the pot a kettle," Bill said with a growl. "But yer fergittin' yer in here just about all the time you ain't chiropracticin', which is just about all the time."

Doc might have said more, but Ed Morley was reminded of a problem he had been having with his neck, and he wondered if Doc might feel of it and see if maybe "they was a kink throwed in it."

As I went to rack the front table and collect the money, Jess Wolf commented about how it was a shame ol' lady Cranford didn't see the value in a boy havin' experience workin' with money regular the way I did.

I didn't say anything, but I hardly ever saw anything bigger than a dollar, and it wasn't at all hard to figure out how to subtract 20 cents from a quarter.

"It 'peers to me like," Jess said, "anyone could see he's gettin' some valuable 'sperience here."

"Valuable experience I reckon," Doc Dykes said as he prepared to look at Ed Morley's neck. "If he ever gets in a situation where he can make a living telling huntin' an' fishin' stories passed down by a bunch of aging prevaricators, then he'll be in great shape."

Immediately Bill motioned me to sit down beside him. Placing a gnarled hand around my shoulder, he asked in a low voice, "Son, did ol' Doc just call us something I ought to know 'bout?" I pretended I hadn't heard, but Preacher Lampkin told him anyway that an aged prevaricator was an old liar. Bill acted relieved. He thought it might have been something worse.

Virgil Halstead had picked up one of my books sitting in its usual place on an empty rack of pop bottles behind the front bench.

"Right here's the kinda thing ah'm aginst. Them there new fangled things they's a teachin'. Readin', ritin' an' rithmetic ain't good enough no more. Why, I went through near six years a schoolin' an we never studied no history."

"Shucks Virgil," Doc Dykes responded, "When you was a boy, they wasn't no history made yet."

Everybody laughed except Virgil, who handed the book to Ol' Bill for his disapproval. "Is they anything in here worth learnin', boy?" .....I told him I was reading something about the Magna Carta.

"Agness Carter!" Ol' Jim sat up straight on his

end of the bench. "I know'd her; she married a Goforth boy down aroun' Tyrone. Nice lookin' girl onc't, but she ain't got a tooth in 'er head now. Her face looks like a week-old deer track!"

"You may not believe it," I said, proud to show off my knowledge of history, "but in France they trained pigs to point, and they would sometimes point birds just like today's bird dogs."

"Now see there," Virgil said indignantly. "They get a young boy to believe any durn thing."

"Ol' Bill aimed at the spittoon and two or three of the Front Bench Regulars moved away. "I guess I'd hafta see that, boy," he said, "afore I'd go to tryin' to train me a young shoat."

Sensing a great deal of skepticism, I pointed out that it was a known scientific fact that pigs were fairly intelligent and possessed a good nose. "Boy, ain't you never been around a hog pen?" Virgil asked. "Ain't nothin' that lives in a hog pen could have a good nose."

"Ain't a bad idea though," Jess said, "a bird-huntin' hog. When the huntin' season is over you could just butcher your bird-hog an' hang 'im in the smoke-house."

Virgil and Rupert Sims were about to shoot a game of snooker, and Bill was thumbing through the history book. "Still can't see it," he said. "A pair of hogs chasin' a rooster pheasant down a fence row."

"Well, I don't know if they hunted pheasants in Europe back then," I said. "I think they mostly used hogs to find truffles with their noses."

It was quiet for awhile, as Bill gazed into the pages of my history book. "I don't reckon I had orta ask what a truffle is," he said.

Virgil was eyeing down a cue stick, trying to find a straight one. Before I could answer, Virgil did. "Truffles!" he said. "Saw hundreds of 'em in the War over in Europe...little ol' pa'tridge-like birds, so dumb you could kill 'em with a stick!"

Virgil began to chalk up, muttering as he did. "Truffles," he snorted. "My milk goat could point truffles!"

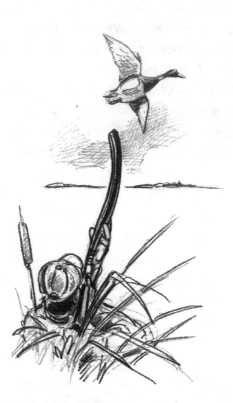

CHAPTER 17

BARBERS AND BENT BARRELS

If there ever was a time you could figure on seeing the pool hall jam-packed, it was Saturday afternoons during November and December. The town was filled with country folk buying groceries and feed for stock. Youngsters were at the matinee at the Melba theatre watching Randolph Scott. And the Regulars were on the front bench.

Usually, Dad and I floated the Piney and hunted ducks on Saturdays. Sometimes, though, we hunted quail with Dad's closest friend, Charlie Hartman. Charlie said he hardly ever went to town with his wife Evelyn because she was awfully bad to go around braggin' about him to total strangers. Charlie was a shy, modest sort, and it's all a man can do to stand around on the street holding a bag of groceries and listening to his wife exaggerate every good point he has and make up some he doesn't have.

I never actually heard Evelyn brag on Charlie. But he did, in fact, have some fine points. No one denied that he trained a bird dog exceptionally well. And I became a dyed-in-the-wool quail hunter at a young age by hunting with Charlie over the best setters and pointers in the county—Ol' Joe, Fanny, Jeannie, and Ace.

I could see why Evelyn was so proud of Charlie...nobody had better bird dogs than he did. I guess Charlie had only one enemy in all of Texas county, and that was a logger from over around Roby who had let his hair get awfully long and shaggy. He told Charlie that he was just sick of paying a dollar-and-a-half every two or three weeks for a haircut.

Charlie sympathized with him and told the fellow that he himself had gone to barber school and would be glad to give the logger a haircut of professional quality for 50 cents. Of course, Charlie never had gone to barber school. For 50 cents, he made that poor fellow ashamed to go outside without a hat.

I also sympathized with the guy, because a dollar-and-a-half was a lot of money for a haircut. You could buy Outdoor Life or Sports Afield for 35 cents and read either one all evening. A haircut took only five minutes. I could buy a chocolate milkshake down at Herron's drugstore soda fountain for 30 cents and make it last longer than that.

But Dad paid for my haircuts and insisted that I have one about once a month. He'd come in the pool hall and say: "Well, shorty, it's about time to get you a haircut or dog tags, one." All the Front Bench Regulars would laugh and slap their knees.

I'd have to take a handful of quarters and go over to Barber Pittman's and sit there all draped up in a big window while every little ol' lady in town walked by and peered in. Then I'd go to the pool hall with my ears two inches lower, smelling like a school teacher—and sit there amongst men who had whiskers longer than my cowlick. I think I'd as soon have had dog tags!

I didn't say as much to Dad, but I expected that kids my age, once they got out on their own, would let their hair grow down to their shoulders.

Six or seven years later, that's exactly what came to pass. Not with me, though. I would come home from college and wind up in the picture window at Barber Pittman's. I never did get real good at rebelling.

It was awfully hard to rebel against Dad, because we hunted and fished together quite a bit on the Piney, and he usually paddled the johnboat and let me sit in front. By the time I got to college, I was still about ten inches shorter and 60 pounds lighter than him. Rebellion in the face of those kinds of odds is sort of foolish. I mean, heck, Washington and his troops crossed the Delaware to face the British against overwhelming odds too, but they probably wouldn't have if they had had to swim.

On occasion, I did rebel against Mom. But then, so did Dad. It was mostly like swimming the Delaware, though. Dad said arguing with Mom was an exercise in futility.

He said things like that which really impressed the Front Bench Regulars. Ol' Jim would try to remember some of the words Dad used so that he could throw them into hunting or fishing stories on occasion.

Ol' Bill thought a lot of my dad because Dad had loaned him his Model 97 Winchester pump gun to go goose hunting over on the Mississippi just before Thanksgiving. Bill said many times that my dad's 97 shotgun was the the finest goose gun he had ever used.

Virgil Halstead said he'd put his old Montgomery Ward 12 gauge pumpgun against any gun, in anybody's hands, as long as it was down the river duck shooting. For years he had hunted ducks on a Gasconade River sandbar just off his brother's farm. The Gasconade had more traffic than the Big Piney, and that kept the ducks stirred up. They'd fly up and down the river, and several hunters enjoyed that kind of Ozark pass shooting.

Virgil got to the point where ducks flying down the river were easy marks. I guess that anything under treetop level was a dead duck when Ol' Virgil pulled down on 'em. But ducks flying up the river were a different story.

Ol' Jim went with him a time or two and he said it was about the strangest thing he'd ever seen, how Virgil could bust northbound ducks about nine times out of ten but just watch those southbound ducks fly off like they were out of range.

Finally, Virgil took the gun to the local gunsmith to get a screw replaced, and the gunsmith figured out what was wrong. Virgil had a bent barrel—a bend that hardly let daylight through to the other end when you looked through it.

Virgil got awful mad when he heard that. He said he knew darn well that his wife had done it years back when she used it to pry open the cellar door. But come to find out, Burley Gooch had owned the gun before Virgil, and Burley claimed that he had never used it for anything but killing rats in Ol' Man Clawson's barn. Burley got ten cents a rat until he broke the stock on the gun. Well Virgil should have known that for ten cents a rat Burley couldn't afford to shoot 'em, he clubbed 'em!

You couldn't feel sorry for Ol' Virgil. Burley got two quarts of blackberry wine for the shotgun and couldn't even remember the trade. No wonder! Burley drank up his end of the barter in a matter of hours so that Virgil couldn't change his mind and renege.

The gunsmith found a used barrel for Virgil's gun. It was straight and not very expensive, the latter being more important to Virgil than the former. The gunsmith intended to keep the old barrel and try to straighten it. Thank heaven he didn't. Virgil hunted three days on his Gasconade sandbar and never killed a duck. He still couldn't hit the upriver ducks, and now he was missing the downriver ducks too.

Well, it was plain to see what happened. Virgil never learned to lead a flying target. But his bent barrel had a built-in lead on all targets moving from left to right because the barrel was bent to the right. Of course, that made Virgil shoot well behind any targets moving right to left. With the new barrel, he was shooting behind everything, whether they were flying up or down the river.

The situation was resolved when the gunsmith agreed to put Virgil's old barrel back on. Ol' Jim advised him to keep the straight barrel for any pond hunting he wanted to do. Jim figured that the bent barrel wouldn't do at all for ducks sitting on the water.

From that point on, though, Virgil was mad at Burley. If he had known his gun had been used for clobbering rats stock first, I don't know if he would have made the trade. But Ol' Burley wasn't quite right. He was near forty, and was still watched over pretty much by his folks.

Just before Thanksgiving he limped into the pool hall like one foot was giving him a great deal of trouble. Ol' Jim asked him what was the matter. Burley told him he reckoned he had a nail in his boot.

"Why shucks boy, why don't ya jus' pull it out?" Jim said, shaking his head.

"Well," Burley said as he leaned back with a sigh, "I just ain't had the time."

After he was gone, everyone had a good laugh about that! Ol' Jim scratched his whiskered chin and shook his head. "Tryin' to talk to that boy is an exercise in fidelity!" he said.

CHAPTER 18

SHORTY AND DOC

I don't remember any of the Front Bench Regulars ever wearing a tie but there were a few snookershooters who were regular visitors that did...Shorty Evans wore a bow tie and Jerald Jeffries and Wade Dykes wore straight ties that went all the way around the collar. Myself, I never wore a tie unless I was forced to, and then it was one of those clip-on types. I figured it cut the risk of being accidentally hung in some kind of machinery or whatever.

I admired men who wore ties however because it made them look so distinguished, and the pool hall needed some of that. Men who wore ties were usually educated and successful types, which gave me some ammunition to use whenever my teachers would say that I'd never amount to nothing if I didn't quit hanging around that pool hall. Shorty Evans was my answer to that. He was one of the best known men in town, with several different successful ventures, including aluminum trolling motor propellors and a line of fishing lures. Shorty Evans was also one of the most outgoing, personable people in our town, and he fished far-off places like Tablerock, Bull Shoals and Norfork lakes, and caught bass that were nearly as big as he was. Shorty wasn't very tall. In fact, as short as I was, he wasn't much taller, maybe just an inch or two over 5 feet. But he stood awfully tall in my eyes. Not only was he a good fisherman, he was one of the best snooker players, and he always seemed to have time to play me a game when I'd challenge him. I didn't win many games against Shorty, but I'd stay close. When we'd get right down to the last few balls and I'd get lined up on a crucial shot Shorty would go to psychological warfare. He' d always say, "Don't let your tail fly up now son," just as I'd get ready to sink the deciding shot. And that would always get me to thinking he knew something I didn't and sure enough, I'd miss.

Shorty was a great golfer too, and he did something for me when I was a kid that I'll never forget. I always made my spending money by guiding float-fishermen or doing odd jobs of some sort or another. But there was good money to be made finding golf balls and

103

reselling them at the local golf course. I'd hunt for lost balls in the weeds along the fairway, and sometimes find 8 or 10 in just a couple of hours. At 25 cents apiece, that could amount to a dollar per hour, and that was a lot back then for a kid. One of the town big shots, the guy that owned the local car dealership, decided I was stealing golf balls. I wasn't.... as a boy I was taught that stealing was worse than anything else a kid could do. My dad would kill me for smoking, drinking or stealing. He would have killed me worse for stealing than anything else. Anyway, I was standing there at the club house confronted by this town big shot and a couple of his cronies about stealing golf balls and just about in tears. Finally they decided that even if I wasn't stealing those balls I was finding out there in the weeds, I didn't have any right to be on the golf course selling them unless I paid green fees. Of course I didn't even know what green fees were, but I knew it was something I'd never be able to pay with the kind of savings account I had. It was about then that Shorty Evans showed up. He pushed everyone to the side with his flambouyant style and asked me if I had any golf balls for sale. In short order he had bought every one I had, and made it a point to tell me to find some more for him. He even told me where he had lost a couple. That was the last time anyone mentioned green fees.

And then there was another good friend of mine who wore a tie...Doc Dykes. He was a gentleman in every sense, intelligent and mild-mannered and very often pestered to death about medical advice. Everybody called Wade Dykes "Doc," because he was a chiropractor, and to many of the Front Bench Regulars that meant he knew about everything from pleuresy to arthritis. He wore that tie and a long overcoat, was always shaven, always had his shoes shined, and played a pretty mean game of snooker too.

Doc Dykes was in the middle of a game one afternoon when Virgil Halstead finally caught up with him. "Yore my only hope, Doc," Virgil said backing him in to a corner. "Ol' Rob, my pointer, has took to snorin' somethin' awful and the little woman says she can't sleep, so he goes or she goes!"

"Man that don't soun' like no big problem," Ol' Bill chipped in, with the attitude of a confirmed bachelor. Everybody laughed but Virgil.

"That woman's been with me forty years or better," he said soberly. "She's gonna be hard to do without."

"Maybe, but I'd still druther have a snorin' dog than a yakkin' woman," Bill answered.

Unperturbed, Virgil pressed Doc for an answer. Between shots, Doc Dykes explained that he wasn't trained to solve dog problems, and no one he knew was trained to solve wife problems. Finally, somebody asked Virgil why ol' Rob couldn't sleep on the porch or in the kitchen maybe. Virgil allowed as how ol' Rob had slept by the bed since he was a puppy...he might snore a bit by the bedside, but anywhere else and he howled and whined all night long.

It became obvious that Doc Dykes wouldn't be able to concentrate on his snooker-playing with Virgil around, so he agreed to help. He told Virgil that after the game he'd go get some medicine to help his wife sleep and stop the dog's snorin'. He came back with two jars of pills, charged Virgil five dollars and played snooker the rest of the evening uninterrupted. I asked him if what he did wasn't illegal.

"Not at all," Doc answered with a smile. The pills for Virgil's wife were nothing but those sleep aids bought over the counter, and the pills for the dog were pet vitamins. Even if Virgil got them switched, it couldn't hurt a thing.

No one could believe it when Virgil came in a couple of days later to announce that Doc Dykes had solved all his problems. When Doc came in that afternoon, I thought ol' Virgil was gonna hug 'im.

"Doc," Virgil said, loud enough for everyone to hear, "I've heard it said that quiropracticers wa'nt real doctors an' not on the level an' all...but I'm hanged if you ain't a miracle worker."

Virgil went on. "Ol' Rob's gonna be needin' his rabies shot soon, an I was wonderin' if..."

Later that evening, Doc was still shooting snooker after most of the Front Bench Regulars had gone home. But he had lost almost every game, and it was clear he didn't have his mind on the snooker table. Finally, after missing an easy shot at the five-ball, he turned around with one hand on his hip, staring into space. "I wonder what made that dog stop snoring?" he asked.

Ol' Bill had the answer, as usual. "Doc," he said, "I'd just call it your bad luck!"

CHAPTER 19

FRIENDS AND ENCOURAGEMENT

On the cover of the November 1961 edition of Outdoor Life was a grizzly standing over a fallen bull elk, roaring a challenge toward a distant cowboy dismounting with rifle in hand.

Erwin Bauer had written an article about float-fishing for adventure, Ted Janes had spun a tale about an Adirondack buck and David Michael Duffy was touting the German wirehair pointer in his column. I was disappointed because there was nothing in the magazine by my favorite writer, Ben East.

I had just turned 14, and life wasn't getting any better. Some of the old timers who warmed the front bench in my dad's pool hall could tell I was down in the dumps. Ol' Bill wanted to know why the long face with duck season and quail season just around the corner.

I explained it to him. I was too short to play basketball and too light to play football. My grades were nothing to brag about, and where I went to school, if you weren't an athlete or a scholar, you weren't much. Ol' Bill said he understood, and it made me feel better to have someone to talk to. But then he went on to say he never had made passin' grades or played on the varsity and it hadn't kept him from gettin' to where he was. For some reason I felt bad again.

"Boy, I reckon it's like the time I had three pointer pups out a that ol' Molly bitch I bought up in Iowa years back," Bill said. "Everybody wanted one pup cause he was the biggest, or the other cause he was the purtiest. The third one kinda got crowded out on every turn, but he had more character than any pup I ever seen. He made a better bird dog than the other two. Just took him longer is all."

I couldn't help but perk up at that. Bill did have a fine pointer dog. "Is Ol' Jake that pup you're talkin' 'bout?" I asked.

"Oh heck no, boy," he said, switching cheeks with his tobacco. "That was years back. Seems like that pup got hit by a cattle truck, if I 'member right."

My shoulders sagged again, but Bill slapped a gnarled hand on my back and said, "Boy, some day it ain't gonna matter who played what an' who made what grades. You'll find somethin' you do better'n anythin' an' you'll work hard at it an' you'll be successful. An' happy too!"

"I don't know," I said. "I don't think there's anything I can do good but hunt and fish."

The old man picked up my magazine and thumbed through it. "Well, then maybe you can be one of these writer fellers someday," he said, stopping at Duffy's column and eyeing the picture of the wirehair pointer. "Don't look like you got to be real smart to do this. Look at this here dog this ol' boy bought." I took the magazine from Bill and began to thumb through it myself. Wouldn't it be something to be a writer, I thought.

"Heck, boy," Ol' Bill added as an afterthought, "now that I think of it, you're probably the best dang 14-year-old pool player in the gol-darn country. Why, you might get famous someday if you work at it. Like that Michigan Fats feller ...a dadblamed professional pool shooter!"

I thought about that awhile. I had an English theme to write, but it would just earn me another C like everything else I wrote. I gave Bill the magazine and reached for a cue stick. It would take an awful lot of practice to get to be the best pool player in the country.

Ronnie Casebeer came in and distracted me before I could get very far along. He was about my age and a pretty fair pool player himself. Ronnie's dad owned the jewelry store next door to the pool hall and he was in there quite often trying to keep from doing whatever chores his dad had given him, like sweeping the floor or washing the store front window. That day he brought in a big fuzzy, real-looking tarantula spider he had found somewhere. It was a fake, of course, but you couldn't tell it. I remember how the two of us marveled over what modern technology could do, making a rubber spider that natural.

We tied a monafilament fishing line to it and ran the line up over the pool hall sign that hung over the sidewalk. Then we strung it through the pool hall door and discovered we could lower that spider onto the sidewalk without being detected at all.

As I explained to my dad later, Ronnie and I had no intention of using that spider to cause any disturbance but from our vantage point, we just failed to see a pair of elderly ladies heading down the sidewalk for Herron's drug store. I assured dad that when we realized that the spider might scare someone, we decided we had better lower it and untie it. As our bad luck would have it, it came down right in front of those two ladies.

One of them wasn't all that alarmed by it. She merely threw her purse at it, and ran screaming into a nearby dress shop. But the other lady climbed atop the trunk of a parked 1956 Oldsmobile, and created something of a display. Ronnie and I had some good times, but the least said about the spider incident, the better.

Then there was Billy Bob Woods, who shot as good a game of snooker for a 14-year-old as you'll find anywhere. When the two of us played snooker, all the old timers stopped to watch. I had one advantage over Billy Bob, there was no pressure on me. If he lost he had to pay, if I lost I didn't. If college recruiters had been looking for snooker players, Billy Bob and I would have been in the limelight, with scholarship offers aplenty. Still and all, Billy Bob's greatest ability wasn't snooker, it was marbles. When we were in the 5th or 6th grade, the school administration had to outlaw "marble-playing-for-keeps" because Billy Bob would end up owning every marble every kid brought to school. There's no telling how many dollars worth of marbles he had in boxes under his bed before they outlawed it, but a big percentage of them were mine.

Many years before my dad bought the poolhall, our house out on Indian Creek burned to the ground, and while it was being rebuilt, we lived in a little house just aways off main street. I didn't know that Billy Bob's dad was an undertaker, nor did I know what an undertaker was. At 7 or 8 years of age, I just hadn't learned anything about funeral homes, except that Billy

Bob lived over one. One evening after school, he and Lonnie McAllister took me to the funeral parlor to visit someone's dearly departed loved one. I wasn't really clear about what we were doing, but I knew that sometimes when you went to another kid's house after school you'd get milk and cookies. There's not a lot I remember about that visit to the funeral home, but I do remember signing the book. Billy Bob said that we needed to sign the book, so I printed my name in the best I could. Then I remember standing on tip-toes to look over the top of that casket. I saw the old gentleman peacefully at rest inside, but I didn't see him very long. I hit the sidewalk running, and my hair didn't lay down completely for several days. And I wouldn't have gone back to Billy Bob's place for all the milk and cookies in town.

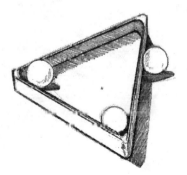

CHAPTER 20

HUNTIN' GOATS AND NEAR MISSES

Mort Jordan, from over around Plato or Roby, I forget which one, tried to sell his dog in the pool hall after each hunting season. Selling the dog before the season would have been smarter, but by that time Mort had forgotten how poorly the dog had hunted the year before and he'd get to thinking he needed a hunting dog for the upcoming season. About January, he'd decide he could do without him again.

I remember one spring night in particular when there was an awful thunderstorm going on outside and everyone had taken refuge in the pool hall, crowded around the front bench. Mort was there trying to sell his dog, and he told us how Ol' Snort, his pointer, always came down on point behind the barn of a certain farm he hunted regularly, a place where Mort had never flushed a bird. Snort was so insistent that Mort usually had to pick him up and carry him away, so he asked around and found out that a civil war soldier had been buried there somewhere in an unmarked grave. His name was Bob White.

It seemed to be an old joke to everyone but me. Mort went on...He said that once, when hunting in another state, his dog worked flawlessly all day, but on each and every point Ol' Snort would lay on his belly, head flat to the ground and tail tucked low. It was really a strange posture for such a stylish, high-headed dog, but later Mort found out why. The land was posted.

At that point the night shaped up as something of a tall-tale contest. As thunder rumbled outside, Jim Stallcup gave his account of his cousin's bird-hunting milk goat.

Jim said he first hunted with his cousin's goat back in the forties and found she would range well, point, and hold both coveys and singles. But Jim said the goat was a far cry from a staunch setter or pointer, lacking the speed and disdaining the retrieve. Still, the goat found four coveys one crisp November morning and Jim was looking forward to a limit before noon.

Suddenly, the goat disappeared. Jim looked for an hour, thinking the goat to be on point somewhere in heavy cover. Finally he walked back to the farmstead to enlist the aid of his cousin. But the goat's owner had a question! Was Jim hunting anywhere in the neighborhood of the old bottom road that led down to the river? Jim allowed as how he was. The farmer shook his head in a bemused fashion.

"Only bad thing about that durn goat," he told cousin Jim, " you just can't hunt her anywheres close to that river. She'd a whole lot druther fish than hunt."

After the laughter subsided, Ev Davis told his favorite dog story about the old boy down by Bucyrus who was courtin' a neighbor lady who had occasion to visit his little cabin back in the woods. She noticed a hole in the floor beside the table, and asked what it was for. The old backwoodsman allowed as to how he dumped all the table scraps and bones through that hole for his dogs sleepin' under the cabin.

"Why, isn't that awfully unsanitary?" the lady

asked.

"No, ma'am, I don't reckon so," the old-timer replied. "I ain't lost a dog yet."

There was more laughter and a bright burst of lightning flashed outside followed by a peel of thunder. About that time Willie Jenkins barged through the door, the brim of his hat dripping rain and his eyes as big as saucers. "I dang near got it," Willie said. "A bolt of lightnin' hit not five feet behind me right then!"

Ol' Bill sat propped on one end of the front bench, his favorite place beside the spittoon already taken. Bill wasn't as tolerant of Willie as everyone else was. "Willie," he said, "if a bolt of lightnin' had hit that close, you'd be sittin' up there at the pearly gates this very minute tryin' to 'splain every'thin' to ol' St. Peter."

Indignant over that remark, Willie began removin' his raincoat and it was plain to see it leaked considerably. Willie was obviously very excited about his close call, and he addressed Bill in a high voice, his words coming faster than usual. "I can tell you this," he said, "it just wasn't my time to go, that's all, cause that lightnin' bolt hit right on my heels."

Preacher Lampkin could see Willie was pretty excited, and he put his arm around Willie's shoulder. "Now Bill," the preacher said, "It could be Willie is right. Obviously the good Lord in his infinite wisdom and mercy saw fit to spare Willie this time!"

Bill walked over to the spittoon and aimed a stream of tobacco juice in its general direction. "Could be," he said as he headed back to his place on the bench. "Then again, maybe he jus' forgot to lead 'im."

CHAPTER 21

BEN EAST, JACK LONDON AND ME

The end of school approached with the speed of an ox-drawn wagon train. Mrs. Rumbaker, my English teacher, had assigned some poems to read that you couldn't make heads nor tails of. I read part of one by some Browning woman and it nearly made me sick to my stomach.

So instead, I read Ben East's account of a moose hunt in Outdoor Life, wondering why English teachers failed to recognize that Ben East and Jack O'Connor made much more sense than Shakespeare.

Things hadn't started out so despairingly. Early in the year my freshman English teacher was pretty close to perfect. Her name was Susan Catlan, just out of college and so beautiful I made a concentrated effort to look and act older. I tried to make Miss Catlan believe I had missed three or four years of schoolin' because of a rare foreign disease of some kind. But when you're thirteen, you look thirteen, and I didn't fool her. It didn't matter, Miss Catlan sort of took a shine to me. She held me after class one day to tell me I was a very good writer for someone who was only thirteen or sixteen or seventeen or however old I really was. I found out she was a great fan of Jack London, and she told me I reminded her a little bit of him when I wrote those hunting dog stories.

I guess that was the only period in all my school

days that I was ready for the school bus an hour before it showed up. But it didn't last. Miss Catlan was fired late in the fall, and Mrs. Rumbaker took her place. From milk and honey to green persimmons!

Mrs. Rumbaker wore glasses and had a deep admiration for Shakespeare. She didn't see any potential in me, joining other teachers in urging me to stay away from the pool hall and the Front Bench Regulars and think about joining the armed services if and when I graduated.

It was about that time that I wrote one of my best dog stories. It concerned a pointer bitch that had whelped a litter of half-wolf puppies. Only two survived, one becoming a fine hunter, and the other reverting to the wild to pillage local livestock. I really believe that if Jack London had been alive at the time (and I didn't know for sure he wasn't), he would have praised that story as being in the mold of his finest work. At the time of course, I knew nothing about plagiarism.

But my English teacher wasn't impressed. She took the best three or four stories from each assignment and read them in class. Always the same three or four students, of course, the ones that sat across the front row and made A's and B's on their report cards, grades I hadn't seen since the second grade.

But my dog story had made some impression, at least. Mrs. Rumbaker wrote a note across the top of it saying something to the effect that I had better never use the word "bitch" again in a story for her class.

She also said she thought my description of the love affair between the pointer and the lobo wolf might have been a bit too descriptive, but what the heck.

120

When you're a writer, you're a writer!

Ol' Bill said it was the best story he had read in years. Several of the Front Bench Regulars who couldn't even read wanted to hear the story, so one evening I read it to them aloud. Everyone was sort of biting their fingernails when I got to the part where the mostly-bird-dog littermate was on point in a sumac thicket and was attacked by his brutal, mostly-wolf brother. I know it may not sound like much of a story at this point, but it got much better at the end, with the mostly-wild brother reforming somewhat. In the end he saved his brother, the bird dog, from being hit on the highway by a tractor trailer and then saved the master's daughter from drowning and being bitten by a rattlesnake.

Ol' Jim said the story was good enough to sell to True Adventure except it wasn't true. He said he couldn't hardly believe how much I had progressed as a writer, remembering the poem I had written on the pool hall's bathroom wall a couple of years before that had gotten me in considerable hot water with my dad.

After everyone heard my dog story that spring evening, it became apparent that most of the Front Bench Regulars had a strong affection for good hunting dogs. Virgil Halstead said when he was a kid, an old moonshiner from down near Slabtown had tried to cross an ice-covered eddy of the Big Piney and fell through. His hound crashed through the ice and pulled the struggling home-brew peddler to safety.

"Only trouble with that," Virgil said sympathetically, "the hound took him back where he was when he was a needin' to cross, so he tries to cross in another place and falls through agin."

"I guess the hound pulled him out again?" Ol' Bill said, somewhat skeptical.

"Yup, he did by golly," Virgil said, "a couple of times I reckon. I guess the old feller finally froze to death cause that houn' didn't know which side a the river the ol' boy's cabin was on."

Everybody laughed as Virgil protested, assuring everyone that it was the gospel truth. I didn't laugh, I could see the makings of a good story there.

That's when I told everybody about Jack London's story about the guy who only had a few matches and his dog, and he was about to freeze if he didn't get a fire built. So he killed his dog to warm his hands and finally froze to death anyway when snow fell on the fire.

It was quiet for a moment, and I could tell no one much liked that story. "Soun's awful gruesome to me," Jess Wolf said, "coulda been a better story if he'd a got a big fire goin', an' the dog went fer help. Don't soun' to me like that London feller knows much about good stories."

"If'n I get out in a blizzard som'ers, an' all I got is three or four matches, I ain't gonna take it out on my poor ol' dog," Ol' Bill said. "If that feller hadn't a froze, they oughta flogged 'im!"

After a spell Ol' Jim sent a stream of tobacco juice toward the spittoon. "Now that I recollec' about it," he said, "a redbone houn' I had years back saved my neck onc't."

If Ol" Jim woulda waited for a minute, I'd have asked how, hungry as I was for more story material. But he didn't wait long.

"He was a layin' on the front porch one evenin' a scratchin' one of his ears with one a his hin' feet whilst me an' this school-teacher type woman was sparkin' in the front yard." Ol' Jim stopped for a minute as serious as he could be, thinkin' back on that turning point. "Wal she looks up there at Ol' Bugler an' she says, "Jim, you're gonna hafta choose between me an' that scroungy ol' houn'!'"

At that the place erupted with laughter, and I never did hear the rest of the story. But it didn't matter. Mrs. Rumbaker never would go for a story like that in English class. But the one about the old moonshiner that froze to death on the wrong side of the river might have potential...especially if I had the hound drown trying to get across the river to save him. If Jack London could have grown up in that pool hall, I thought to myself, he might have been as famous as ol' Robert Shakespeare hisself.

CHAPTER 22

ARVELL LANGLEY'S DOG

Arvell Langley ran a community store over on the other side of Bucyrus, one of those little country stores with a gas pump and a potbellied stove where you could get a bologna and cheese sandwich with mayonnaise made while you wait for only a quarter.

Arvell had a wife and five or six little kids, and he was as easygoing and mild-mannered as anyone who ever came in the pool hall, though he only showed up on Saturdays while the wife looked at dress material or bought feed for the chickens.

Arvell found a pretty little liver-and-white pointer bitch in the fall of 1961, half-starved and apparently pretty much abused by someone. After he nursed her back to health, he made the mistake of telling someone that she was a good bird dog. Until then, no one had made any effort to claim the dog despite an honest effort on Arvell's part to find the owner.

One Saturday he brought the little pointer into town in the back of his pickup. Arvell hadn't been in the pool hall more than fifteen minutes when Lutie Scruggs came stompin' in with his cousin Skeeter, the two of them vowing to whip the feller who had stolen Lutie's dog—the pointer sittin' in the back of that pickup just outside.

A couple of no-goods, those two were downright mean when they got together. Dad had run both of them out of our place before—and would again if he caught them in there. But with Dad gone, Lutie was feeling his oats.

Arvell meekly allowed as how he had tried to find the dog's owner, so before Lutie was going to reclaim the pointer, he would have to bring the law in with him. At that Lutie ruffled up and said that he and Skeeter might just haul Arvell out and put a knot on his head before they took the dog. Most of the Front Bench Regulars were three times Lutie's age, but Ol' Bill pointed out that a dozen old-timers within reach of several twenty-ounce cue sticks made it unlikely that Arvell would be gettin' hauled out in the street by anybody. Ol' Jim was already rollin' up his sleeves, and Jess and Herschel, Ev, Jack, Charlie and several others seemed ready to back him.

I'll tell you, I was scared! Dad and Grandpa were gone, so there wasn't anyone around to defuse the situation. But Ol' Bill seemed to have a solution. He rubbed his chin and said that he reckoned the dispute should be settled in a gentlemanly manner, with Arvell and Lutie shooting a game of snooker and the winner taking the dog.

I winced. Arvell was only a mediocre snooker player, but Lutie played for money over at Mountain Grove. I figured Arvell would be hard pressed to beat Lutie one game out of five. But Ol" Bill took him aside and talked to him for a minute or so, and I'll be dad-blamed if he didn't agree to it. In fact, it was Ol' Bill who commenced to settin' up the rules and swearin' both to be honorable men and accept the outcome.

I noticed that Arvell's hands were shaking when

126

he shot, but somehow he got off to a pretty good start. Lutie was cocky and cool. He methodically ran off strings of fifteen or twenty points at a time, building up a good lead.

He never noticed when Ol' Bill slipped out to get some tobacco, what with the big crowd that had gathered. Bill was back and the game was half over when the phone rang and a man's voice I had never heard before asked for Lutie Scruggs.

Lutie seemed really surprised to be getting a call, and we noticed him nodding and listening intently with the receiver pressed close to his ear. When he returned to the table, leading by twenty points, it was plain that Lutie had something important on his mind. He was fidgety and complained that Arvell was taking too long to shoot.

Coached by Ol' Bill, Arvell had calmed considerably. He became very deliberate, slowly cutting into the lead. Lutie, meanwhile, began to perspire a little, shooting carelessly and quickly, obviously losing his concentration. He missed an easy shot, then scratched on the six ball. With his lead cut to only five or six, Lutie finally just hung up his cue and told Arvell that the dog was not worth the effort. In a matter of seconds, he and Skeeter were out the door.

There was cheering and back-slapping. Arvell, brought near to tears with his good fortune, bought Nehi sodas for everyone . I wondered then how a man could grow so fond of a stray dog, but I would learn that in later years.

I would also learn just what happened that day. The mysterious voice on the phone was that of the corner druggist who owed Ol' Bill a favor. He had told Lutie he was the new game warden and that he had a search warrant to find out if an illegal deer was in Lutie's smokehouse as someone had reported. He said it would take him about 45 minutes to get to Lutie's place, and he'd wait there for him. Lutie could get home in 25 minutes, so he decided that there was little point in finishing the game with such pressing matters waiting.

Arvell Langley made a fine bird dog out of that pointer. Lutie Scruggs left the Ozarks and was killed in a car accident a year or so later up around Kansas City.

I guess he had changed for the better, though. Word had it that one Saturday afternoon a poor family that lived down the road from the Scruggs' place was surprised to see Lutie drive up in a cloud of dust and leave them nearly a whole, frozen deer carcass. He seemed to be in a hurry, they said. Didn't even hang around to say, "You're welcome."

CHAPTER 23

ONE LEG AND A GOOD MULE

During the early summer, the pool room wasn't the most popular place in Texas County. That was our slowest time of the year. The Front Bench Regulars thinned out a bit; part of them devoting more of their spare time to fishing.

Jess Wolf was one who was always around though, and when there weren't many folks to compete with, he was more talkative. One morning I helped Grandpa McNew open up just after sunrise and in the cool of the morning, Ol' Jess walked in to find the front bench completely empty except for me and the latest issue of Outdoor Life.

I showed him the two-page painting of a pair of pointers and a covey rise. "Wouldn't you like to be in the middle of that come November?" I asked.

Jess sat down on the bench and crossed his legs. "I seen a fine dog or two in my day," he said. "Why I 'member a dog my old uncle had what could smell a quail through a grass fire. My uncle had to sell him cause the darn dog hated his mule so bad."

I wasn't sure I heard that right. So I asked why a bird dog had to be sold because he hated mules. Jess would have told me anyway. "My uncle lost his leg in World War I," he said. "Got drunk one night on leave from boot camp...got run over by a train, I think...anyhow that ain't important. Loved to hunt quail don't you know, but he couldn't with just one leg, so he bought hisself a fence-jumpin' mule some coon hunter had broke, and took to bird huntin' on that mule."

"And the dog hated the mule so he had to sell 'im," I said, finally getting the gist of it.

"Yeah, I reckon that's the way it was all right," Jess said rubbing his chin. "Then he got hisself a fine little setter and I tell you, them three was death on quail. Course the mule was cantankerous...he'd balk ever now and then and my old uncle would grab one of those long ears and bite like heck...only way he could get that mule to behave. I can't remember when that mule didn't have one ear or t'other all chawed to pieces!"

"I can't help but feel sorry for the mule," I said.

"I reckon so," Jess sighed. "I doubt that any mule likes huntin' quail all that much...an' course he was dang near deaf from all that shootin' right over his head."

The screen door slammed, and Billy Bob Woods came in wanting to shoot a game of snooker. He was my age, the only two kids my age who came in the pool hall to shoot snooker was Billy Bob and Bobby Goodman. The three of us were the best dang 14-year-old snooker players in southern Missouri.

"My uncle gave up quail huntin' when he got older," Jess said as I picked out a cue stick. "Sold his dog an just quit."

"I guess he lost all his teeth and couldn't make that mule behave?" I said, probably ruining Jess' story.

Jess took off his cap and shook his bald head. "Shucks boy, a man with false teeth can bite a mule's ear can't he?" Jess acted a little irritated.

Here I was making light of a serious situation. "Got to where there wa'nt no quail hardly," he said, as Billy Bob lined up the cue ball to break. "So my uncle and that mule took to wadin' the creek jump-shootin' ducks..."

Billy Bob scattered the balls all over the table and it was my turn to shoot. "I guess he got a duck-fetchin' dog then?" I said as I lined up an easy shot.

"Never had to," Jess was quick to answer, " but he was the only duck hunter I ever knowed that carried a dip net on his mule.

CHAPTER 24

POLITICS

Ol' Bill gave me some good advice just before election time. "Always be honest an' upright boy," he told me in a serious, somber tone, "cause it's the way to live, an' if you go a'gin ever'thing good and decent, you'll wind up in jail 'bout half the time."

He was quiet, letting me think about that as he pulled out a plug of tobacco and began to carve on it with an old Barlow knife. "Course if you just can't do it...if it's in yer nature to lie an' cheat an' steal an' live a low-down life, there's one way to stay outa jail," he said, working hard to chew up that plug of tobacco and talk at the same time.

He knew I'd ask how, and I did.

"Well, boy," he said, propping his right foot on the spittoon trying to get his old knife in the right pocket, "get into politics. If you can stand the taste of it, there ain't much risk of payin' fer yer crimes."

Ol' Bill was upset a little because the big issue in local politics that year was whether or not to turn Main Street into a one-way street. The pool hall sat right smack in the center of town, on Main Street, of course. The proposed change would have Main Street traffic running north.

As luck would have it, Bill lived out north of town, and the one-way street would require him to drive to the south end of town and come back up Main Street to the pool hall. He figured it amounted to a quarter mile extra travel per each trip to town, and with gasoline at twenty cents a gallon, Ol' Bill could see himself spending several dollars more per year just to come to the pool hall. He asked me if I could figure up just how much it might come to. I tried, but couldn't...and finally told him that it must take algebra or geometry and I hadn't learned either. I was having problems with simple arithimetic.

The proposal affected most all the Front Bench Regulars in some way or another, and as was always the case when a change of any kind was in the offing, they were all "ag'in it."

Herschel Foyt was downright mad about the whole idea, and had good reason to be. Hershel's dog, Trooper, was an aging brown and white pointer. And according to Hershel he was a fine bird dog in his day, worth $10 or $15. Herschel raised him from a pup, and old Trooper went everywhere with his owner, riding in the back of the pickup. Some said that Hershel only took Trooper along because he was afraid to leave the dog at home where he would be at the mercy of Hershel's wife, who had threatened to poison the pointer on ocasion.

Herschel always denied that. He said his wife had threatened to poison him too, but she never had done it! He said he let the old dog ride along as a reward for all those years of finding and fetching bobwhites. To Herschel the trouble with a one-way street was obvious. Angle parking put the back end of his pickup out in direct sunlight, whereas parallel parking offered shade. Hot sunlight would sap his dog's energy and ruin his nose, Herschel said, and he wouldn't stand for it! He firmly believed it was all the work of old lady Foster who owned the West Side Cafe. She had threatened to go to the city council several months before as the result of a confrontation with Herschel about parking in front of her restaurant. She said Trooper was bad for her business, having ruined the appetites of several customers by hanging over the side of Hershels pickup, peering in through the plate glass window at folks eating steaks and eggs and pecan pie, and drooling all over the sidewalk.

Hershel said he wasn't one to stick his foot in front of the wheels of progress but he couldn't stand by and watch a good bird dog be ruined by a city ordinance. Looking back, I can't remember if the Front Bench Regulars ever mustered enough political power to change anything at city hall. Main street was made into a one-way street for a time and then changed back. And as for old Hershel and his dog, I can't remember for sure, but I believe his wife did, in fact, poison both of them.

But the Front Bench Regulars always believed in the political process. They never made a difference in anything, but they always thought they could. As election time grew closer, there were some big arguments around the front bench over politics. Ol' Bill said that almost every fight between young men is over money or women, and almost every fight between old men is over religion or politics.

"When a feller completely fails at ever'thing," Bill told me one evening in the fall, "he usually gets into politics."

We didn't get many elected officials in the pool hall, but Lemuel Curtis, the County Clerk, came in once, handing out cards and asking for support in the upcoming election. Mr. Curtis had been in office for many years, but I guess he was expecting a close race from a new challenger.

He gave poor Willie Jenkins a card, too. Mr. Curtis knew Willie wasn't quite right, but he wanted to be polite, I guess. Willie didn't even know when election day was, but he was impressed by that card, and tickled that someone would give him that kind of attention.

"I'll vote fer ya, Mister," Willie said with that grin

he was almost never without. "Ol' Bill says we need to get rid of all them worthless no-accounts we got in there now."

Mr. Curtis was smiling as the screen door slammed behind him, but Bill's face was red as a snooker ball. I'm sure that everyone was choking back a laugh and I'm just as sure Ol' Bill was considering choking Willie.

Eventually we got a visit from a real prize winner. He was runnin' for "state guvamint" as Bill put it. The guy was soft and fat, way out of place in that new flannel shirt he had on. I figured he had a tie under it.

Most of the Front Bench Regulars detested that man. Jess Wolf said it best when he declared, "Choosin' between two of them kind of fellers is like trying to choose between eatin' a coot or shitepoke fer supper."

The legislator got around to everyone, askin' for their support. When he got to Bill, he stood way back aways from the spittoon while he shook his hand and vowed that he'd do his best to keep the Conservation Department from placing any further hunting and fishing restrictions on "folks like us."

"I'm somethin' of an outdoorsman myself," he told Bill. "Spent many a night chasin' coons and muskrats through hills behind a good hound."

There were a few subdued snickers here and there. Whoever heard of chasin' muskrats through the hills with a hound.

With a grin on his face and a twinkle in his eye, Ol' Bill decided to have a bit of fun. "Well now tell me," he said, aiming a spray of tobacco juice toward the spittoon as the lawmaker took a step back to protect his $40 shoes, "as a dog man, do you prefer a fine English setter for quail, or are you one of them fellers that's partial to them ol' long rangin', hard-headed, fuel-burnin' pointers?"

The politician was taken aback for only a moment. Then he regained his composure, slapped Ol' Bill on the back, and said that if he couldn't own a fine setter, he'd as soon hunt quail with a stockdog.

Bill shook his head, and a look of disappointment came across his leathery face. Staring at an ongoing snooker game, he said with a sigh, "I dunno, I've always favored them pointers myself."

There were some chuckles, and the politician, sensing that he wasn't gaining any votes here, grinned as if he too appreciated the joke, and sidled toward the door.

But Willie Jenkins stopped him, sticking out his hand with a great air of importance. "You got my vote, Mister," he said in his high-pitched voice.

I learned a lot about politics over the years listening to the Front Bench Regulars. Old Bill was right about about most of it. He said the smartest folks held onto their beliefs and voted their conscience and made everybody wonder what political party they were sided with. My Grandpa McNew was wiser yet. He told me to take a good hard look at the people, and vote for the best one runnin'. And he said I'd probably have more friends in life if all the Democrats thought I was a Democrat, and the Republicans thought I was a Republican.

CHAPTER 25

A NIGHT ON THE PINEY

Back in the summer of '63, Roy Wayne Jones and I spent quite a few nights camped on the river and running trotlines, intent upon catching big flathead catfish. We caught a few, too. In fact, for a pair of 14-year-olds, we did pretty well.

Every sleepless night spent on a Big Piney gravel bar waiting to run the lines was a great adventure—

except for the time that Roy Wayne's grandpa, old Joe Throgmorton went along. Compared to Joe, most of the Front Bench Regulars were men of distinction. Joe was sort of lazy and was a bad influence on growing boys. The tobacco he chewed, the whiskers he shaved only once a month, and the tall stories that flowed from him for hours on end made him something of a loner. But folks always said Ol' Joe had a good heart, and could be trusted when the chips were down.

Ol' Joe just kept on after Roy Wayne and me about fishing, until finally we said we'd go. He had a new johnboat he had built, and he said he'd take that fine boat if we would take care of all the gear.

So there we were, paddlin' down the McKinney eddy one evening in late July in a johnboat that looked like a feed trough that had little fountains in the bottom of it.

Joe sat in the middle, holding his arm, while Roy Wayne and I huffed away on the paddles trying to get to our gravelbar campsite before we sank. "Gol-darn arm-a-mine's jest plumb dead with the rumatiz," he kept sayin'. "Boys, don't she run true, though! Finest boat ah ever built. Ah jes' b'lieve ah'll paddle 'er back up the river tomorrer mahself if'n ah kin git the feelin' back in this here arm."

Roy Wayne and I were to set trotlines and seine the bait, while old Joe set up the canvas lean-to and fixed supper. When we were finished about dark, we found Joe holding his arm again, groaning in pain. One of our cans of beans had been emptied, half the bologna was gone, and the bed rolls and canvas lean-to were piled there on the gravel bar.

As we did his job for him, he tried to make us feel good about it. "Boys, ah wisht ah wuz th' man right now I wuz when I wuz yore age," he told us in his I-can't-hardly-go-on-no-further voice. "Why, I 'member takin' fifty-pounder yaller cats outa this very hole when I waren't mor'n 12 y'ar old..."

Intent on getting the lean-to up, I lost most of the story, but he finished as we gathered wood for a fire.

"...yes sir, boys, folks come from all over jes' to see that big catfish. Why they wuz camped out on the courthouse lawn from Roby and Plato an' Bucyrus an'..."

We ate the last of the bologna and crackers as he got off on another story, and unrolled damp blankets by the campfire light as he continued.

"...so ol' man Macumber, he says, 'Joe, I lost me a calf an' two young goats to that ol' mountain lion, an I know yore the onliest man in these parts that kin...'"

I would like to remember us dozing off to sleep as Ol' Joe told another story before the dying campfire, but such was not our luck. I do remember the dampness of my blankets, the pair of rocks beneath them that grew slowly as the night progressed, and the snoring that quieted everything from tree frogs to whippoorwills. It started way down deep and ended in a whistle, folowed by a series of gasps and moans that made it sound as if he were dyin'. Unfortunately he didn't, and each snore was followed by another equally as bad.

Mercifully, dawn came to the Piney, and we staggered bleary-eyed to the half-filled johnboat with Ol' Joe expounding on the beauty of the river at dawn and the good feeling it gave a man to arise with the creatures of the forest.

We had a fair-sized catfish on the trotline, 8 or 10 pounds anyway. Joe's dead arm came to life as he offered to land the fish himself or crack our heads together if he couldn't, whichever we preferred. So we let him try, and he lost it.

Back in town, he cornered some fellows in the pool hall and told them about the big catfish that had straightened out the hook just as he prepared to let us land it. Thirty pounds or better, he said it was.

Roy Wayne and I tried to sneak out before he saw us come in, but we were too late. He pulled us to the side and explained in his boys-I-hate-to-do-it voice, "Reckon ah'll not git to go with you-uns tonight." Roy Wayne's sagging face brightened as we tried to look disappointed.

"Problem is," Ol' Joe went on, "ah jes' can't sleep on them ol' gravel bars like ah use ter could."

We headed for the soda fountain at the corner drug store, with Ol' Joe on our heels, tellin' us where we oughta set our lines next. We slurped away on a pair of cherry cokes, heads down, trying to act like we didn't know who the guy was sittin' on that stool gesturing wildly with his hands, recalling a story that everyone could hear.

"...so ah figgers right off, it'll take a dad blamed hay hook to hold this ol' catfish, an ah'm the man that kin..."

CHAPTER 26

SPELUNKERS

I don't want to give anyone the idea that I didn't have any type of life outside the pool hall. Shucks no. I had cousins, so many of 'em I can't remember 'em all without a special effort.

Anyway, the pool hall was closed on Sunday and I went to church with my cousins out at Brown Hill, and then on Sunday afternoon we'd go fishing or exploring or something exciting. Part of the time we hunted and explored caves along the Big Piney. That's when I first heard the term "spelunking."

One of the fellows said 'spelunking' meant finding lost and buried treasure. The main purpose of our group was finding and exploring caves, but we all agreed that should we come across any treasure, we'd pack it on home. So the seven of us voted to name our organization the Big Piney Cave Exploring and Spelunking Association. It was an outgrowth of the Big Piney Coon-Hunters Association, which fizzled out in the winter of 1961 because of a lack of good coon-hounds and the difficulty encountered in splitting the proceeds of one possum-hide per week or so between seven boys. We ranged in age from 11 to 14. I had just turned 14 and so had my cousin, Butch. His brothers were 13-year-old Dave and 11-year-old Darb. Then there were Tom and his brother Roy Wayne, and Jerry, all of them about the same age. Your age had something to do with how you fared in the regular Friday night penny-ante poker game. Sometimes an older boy would win as much as 25 or 30 cents and a younger member could lose nearly that much, with the exception of Dave, who always lost ten cents in the first half hour and quit mad.

Our group couldn't do much on the meager allowances of country boys. But coons and caves and Friday night meetings were within our means. We got along well, except for Dave and Darb, the Cain and Abel of the Ozarks.

Their running feud was always a problem. Like on the Sunday afternoon we set forth to explore a large sink hole in search of a gold shipment hidden during the civil war. Jerry claimed rebel troops had stolen the gold, hidden it in a sink hole in the area and shortly thereafter were wiped out by an epidemic of yellow fever.

We dropped a rope into that dark yawning hole, tied it to a nearby tree and left Darb there to go for help if there was no bottom in the thing. The gold was gone, of course, and so was the rope when we decided to climb out. We learned that Dave had called Darb a choice name or two as he descended, and now the younger brother expected a great deal of crawling and begging from the elder.

Dave chose to hurl insults and profanity toward the mouth of that hole, growing deeper and darker by the moment. Butch and Tom quickly grabbed and gagged him, and I begged Darb to reconsider over Dave's muffled promises of imminent disaster. I finally promised that if he would allow the rest of us to climb out, we would leave Dave in that sink hole until he rotted or found the gold.

We broke our promise to Darb, and there was a fight afterward, but there always was anyway. The knots on their heads just shifted positions from week to week. They fought amongst each other, but you had both of them to deal with if you crossed one or the other.

One Sunday afternoon we found a cave just big enough to crawl into on hands and knees. All seven of us proceeded to find the end of the thing, with Darb and Dave well separated and me leading the single file progression.

After what seemed like a mile of crawling, the space got smaller and wetter, and my knees more tender. I began to think of earthquakes and cave-ins and quickly began asking myself what I was doing there. It took some thinking. If I tried to talk everybody into retreating, I'd be an outcast, made light of by my comrades. So I stopped and began to mutter under my breath. Everyone began to ask what the problem was. Knowing no one could see past me, I described a snarling, defensive wildcat just ahead.

"Aw, don't worry," I said reassuringly, "I think we can get past him if we...dad-blamed it he ain't foamin' at the mouth!" Most of our members were retreating in reverse without further question, so I joined them. I think Butch always knew that I made up that wildcat, but he never said anything. He was the best friend I ever had back then that was my age, and whatever problems developed we were there to help each other out. That all ended of course, when Butch got a girlfriend a year or two later. None of us could figure out why he'd rather be with her than us.

But before we grew up, in that year or so of cave

exploring, we had some shining times. We never found any treasure, but there was a cave where we found arrowheads lying on top of the dry floor, and there was a cave none of us will ever forget that surely few modern men had seen. We squeezed through a small entrance one Sunday afternoon to find a large stream flowing way back in that Ozark hillside, with blind salamanders and hundreds of bats. The room was high and domed, like a cathedral of some kind, and the sparkling colored rock formations like great thin elephant ears. There wasn't a broken formation anywhere, and we left it as we found it, each promising never to tell another soul of its whereabouts.

Cave exploring was only one of many things to do back in those days. We were too busy enjoying any spare time we had to give much thought to things that would get us in trouble.

I feel sorry for youngsters who grow up with only asphalt and cement to explore, without wild places to be young in. Youngsters who never experience and deal with nature never have the right perspective on life. We were lucky kids, we had dads and uncles and grandfathers and clean creeks to swim in and caves to explore and fish to catch. Church on Sunday morning and high adventure on Sunday afternoon!

150

COACH AND THE SHOTGUN

Coach Wilkens wasn't one of the Front Bench Regulars; he didn't have time to sit around and chew tobacco and worry about why there weren't as many quail as there once was.

But Coach did come in the pool hall quite often, and that's something no other teacher did. Most of the others thought I would become a juvenile delinquent because of my association with characters like Ol' Bill and Jess Wolf and Jim Stallcup and the rest of the Front Bench Regulars. Coach said there were a lot of ways to get educated. He even warned me once that my dad was coming down the street in time for me to throw my outdoor magazine behind the soda machine and get my school books out.

Coach said I shouldn't worry about not being a basketball player, since I might be the best 14-year-old snooker player in all of southern Missouri and one of the best duck hunters on the Big Piney for my age.

You can see why I liked Coach Wilkens. But he wasn't as experienced as the Front Bench Regulars, and they took advantage of that. J.W. Roberts, a farmer from down around Tyrone or Solo somewhere, had an old shotgun he had been trying to sell for $40. It was an old double-barrel with a cracked fore-end and the blueing was worn. It didn't even have hammers to make it pretty, and one firing pin was worn too short, causing that barrel to fire only about half the time.

Coach made the mistake of saying he'd like to get an old double-barrel and the old timers in the pool hall were quick to let J.W. know. The place was darn-near packed that Friday night when Coach stopped by to look at J.W.'s old gun. The place reminded me of a limb full of chicken hawks. I wished I could warn Coach, but danged if his eyes didn't light up when he saw that gun.

"Seen one just like it kill a goose at a hundred yards or better," Jim Stallcup chipped in as J.W. extolled the virtues of the double barrel. Coach said he couldn't hardly make out the brand name, but J.W. said he knew it well. Some brothers in the gun business made those guns years ago, then broke up to form new companies, as he'd heard. Winchester and Remington, he thought.

Coach said $75 was awful high. J.W. said because of his interest in the educational system, he'd take $50 but Coach ought to be ashamed of himself, knowing the plight of farmers. Rupert Sims, another farmer, said he wished he had $50. He shook his head, remembering when J.W. had given nearly "two hunnert dollars" for that very gun at his uncle's auction. Of course, everyone knew J.W. had traded a pair of worn out old tires for the gun, a year before, right there in the pool hall.

When Coach finally agreed to pay J.W. $5 a month for the next ten months, Ol' Bill just sat there on the bench with his feet propped on the spittoon, shaking his head. Coach Wilkens finally left, proudly clutching his new gun, and J.W. bought all the Front

Bench Regulars a round of Orange Crush and Grape Nehi to celebrate. Later, after I had swept the floor and covered the tables, Ol' Bill and I sat waiting for Dad to come by and close up.

"I wouldn't feel sorry for that there Coach feller," Ol' Bill told me. "He'll probably make ten bucks off that ol' gun once he gets to school. That place is full o' folks just like him..., principals and English teachers an' the like."

"It just don't seem right though," I said, sighing. "Seems like Coach would know better, as much as he hunts. Maybe if it was a Winchester or a Remington or an Ithaca it wouldn't be too bad, but who ever

CHAPTER 28

A FINAL FAREWELL

The pool hall sat at the very center of town on the east side of Main Street. The building is still there, but it's now an accounting firm owned by a lady I went to school with...Rose Hicks Ward. In fact she was 13 or 14 the same time as I was, and her daddy came in the pool hall on occasion too, as I remember. Rose has changed things quite a bit, but inside, the old radiators are still there and so is the huge window fan that helped clear the smoke. Awhile back I revisited the place. I could almost hear the click of billiard balls and see Ol' Bill there on the front bench, his feet propped on the spittoon with his arms across his knees, always leaning forward as if intently studying something.

Bill had been my grandfather's trapping partner years back, and that man spent a tremendous amount of time on the Piney River, hunting, trapping, and trotlining. He was gruff and cynical and intolerant, but in charge as far as the front bench was concerned. He was liked and respected despite his stern countenance, because when he talked hunting, fishing, or trapping, everyone knew he had done what he talked about. But he got into other areas quite often, and he made it plain that he had little use for Russians, politicians, and greenhorns.

Jess Wolf was one of my favorite people. I didn't change his name, as I have most of the others...maybe because Ol' Jess was someone special to me. He'd doze off on the bench and I'd take his cap from his head without awakening him and then hide it. When he'd wake up, he'd look for it for ten minutes or so, ranting and raving because they let a dad-blamed kid work in a pool hall and cause nothing but trouble. I'd deny I ever touched his cap, of course, while everyone else would grin and snicker and swear that they hadn't even noticed he had one on.

Jess and General Rollins once had a disagreement over religion out on the street, and the two old men took a swing or two at one another before the rhubarb was broken up by the lady who ran the dress shop.

For awhile after that I referred to Jess as Sonny Liston and General as Floyd Patterson. Jess took it all in fun, but not General. He never cared much for me, saying often, "If I had a kid like you, I'd keep him in a cage!"

Ol' Jim was another one I enjoyed listening to. He was the darndest bullshooter we ever had in the pool hall. No doubt, Jim made up things he had never seen or done, but it was fun to listen to those stories. He had one redeeming quality. He would always support any kind of wild story, declaring that he'd seen the same thing happen and giving a half-dozen reasons why he believed the whole doggone tale, no matter what it was.

But there were a dozen or so more "Regulars," and I could write volumes about each. Clad in overalls and flannel shirts, brogan shoes and caps with ear flaps, they were some of the most colorful old timers ever assembled in one place. Some were rivermen, some were farmers, but they all hunted and fished—or talked about it like they did—and I couldn't get enough of it.

There was a great deal of wisdom on that front bench, though I didn't recognize it at the time. When you are young, you don't see the difference in intelligence and wisdom. But I began to understand as I grew older. Once, when things were slow in the pool hall, Ol' Bill and I were watching some men pouring a cement sidewalk across the street in front of the Post Office.

"Isn't it something," I said, "that men can make something stronger than nature!"

Ol' Bill shook his head in disagreement. "Not stronger, boy. Nothing's stronger than Ol' Mother Nature...she's just a mite slower than the eye can see."

When I looked puzzled, he went on. "I can show you a sidewalk that looked as pretty an' smooth as that'n when they first made it, back years ago. Now it's all cracked an' buckled, an' they's weeds growin' up around the busted chunks."

Ol' Bill reached for his twist of tobacco and knife, and I listened.

"I wouldn't a bleeved such a thing when I was a youngster," he said as he whittled off a chunk of chewing tobacco. "But boy, if you give it time, a little ol' sprout will bust the hardest cement."

I didn't say anything, and Bill thought for a moment before he went on, as if maybe he was telling me something he had just discovered for himself.

"You don't realize about them sorta things til you've put on lots a years, boy, but I've seen the river move gravelbars over the years, just a few rocks at a

157

time. An' I've watched an oak saplin' grow up out of a rot'nin' log an' remembered when that log was a live tree, growin' straight an' strong.

"I always sorter liked this country the way the good Lord made it, boy," he said. "But most folks figger they can make it better, so here comes this farmer an' he cuts all the trees, an' shoots all the hawks an' hoot owls, an' lets his cows foul up the river, an' makes it so they can't hardly nothin' live but him, an' he ain't livin' all that good neither."

"Then he gets old an' dies and in time ever'thing he built rots away, ever' hole he dug fills in, and ever' fence he built falls down. There'll be a day when ever'thing he lived for is forgotten, and the river will be clear agin, an' the trees tall an' the hawks an' the hoot owls livin' jus' like they did afore he came along."

Ol' Bill sensed that it all might be a little confusing, so he stood up and put a hand on my shoulder. "Jus' look out there at Main Street, boy," he said with a a solemn air, "an' take my word for it. They was oak trees an' hickories growin' there once...an' there will be agin."

In time, the cement buckles, and a sprout becomes a saplin', and the saplin' becomes a tree. A boy grows to manhood, slowly but surely. The years passed and I went away to college. My dad sold the pool hall, an' within' a couple of years they closed it. The Front Bench Regulars disbanded and drifted off, one by one into nowhere.

I saw a few of my old friends again from time to time on those occasions when I returned home to fish and hunt the Big Piney and visit my family. And then, from time to time in her letters, my mom would tell me, one by one, of the passing of the men I had once known so well.

Ev Davis, Doc Dykes, Jess Wolf, Herschel Foyt, and Virgil Halstead. Ol' Jim Stallcup, and Ol' Bill too, in his seventies. He was buried one winter afternoon while I sat in a college classroom, listening to an obnoxious college professor who knew for sure that he and Charles Darwin had the answer to everything. He was bent on convincing young minds that their parent's teachings and small town attitudes were out of style.

"You're a true product of the Ozarks," that professor told me, "backward, stubborn, and set in your ways, like those old men in overalls who sit whittling on courtyard benches."

I looked him in the eye and I thanked him for that. And I asked him if he'd ever set a trotline. I'll never forget the puzzled look on his face when he asked what a trotline was. Intelligence......but no wisdom!

In small cemeteries on wooded hillsides scattered throughout the Big Piney watershed, the Front Bench Regulars are buried. I like to think God gave them a place where they can be together to catch fish and swap stories and laugh about some of the things that thirteen-year-old kid did in the pool hall back in the hills.

I hope that they all know how much they meant to me, and how much I learned from them. Even now, I can still hear them, and see them, over the clack of billiard balls and the slamming of the screen door; the laughter, the arguments, the stories. True products of the Ozarks, each and every one, and proud of it. So am

Other books by Larry Dablemont

–Ain't No Such Animal

–Greatest Wild Gobblers
Lessons learned from Old Timers and Old Toms

–Memories From A Misty Morning Marsh
A Duck Hunting Treasury

–Rivers to Run
How to Float & Enjoy the Streams of the Midwest

–An Old Fashioned Fisherman
Angling Experiences and Adventures

For more information write to:

Lightnin' Ridge Books

Box 22, Bolivar, Missouri 65613